CHRISTMAS GIFTS of GOOD TASTE

EDITORIAL STAFF

Vice President and Editor-in-Chief: Anne Van Wagner Childs
Executive Director: Sandra Graham Case
Editorial Director: Susan Frantz Wiles
Publications Director: Carla Bentley
Creative Art Director: Gloria Bearden
Senior Graphics Art Director: Melinda Stout

DESIGN
Design Director: Patricia Wallenfang Sowers
Designers: Katherine Prince Horton, Sandra Spotts Ritchie,
 Linda Diehl Tiano, Rebecca Sunwall Werle, and Anne Pulliam Stocks
Executive Assistant: Billie Steward

FOODS
Foods Editor: Celia Fahr Harkey, R.D.
Assistant Foods Editor: Jane Kenner Prather
Test Kitchen Home Economist: Rose Glass Klein
Test Kitchen Coordinator: Nora Faye Taylor

TECHNICAL
Managing Editor: Kathy Rose Bradley
Senior Technical Writer: Briget Julia Laskowski
Technical Writer: Margaret F. Cox
Technical Associates: Leslie Schick Gorrell and Carol V. Rye

EDITORIAL
Managing Edito
Senior Associat
Associate Editor: Terri Leming Davidson
Assistant Editors: Robyn Sheffield-Edwards and
 Darla Burdette Kelsay
Copy Editor: Laura Lee Weland

ART
Book/Magazine Graphics Art Director: Diane M. Hugo
Senior Production Graphics Artist: Michael A. Spigner
Photography Stylist: Karen Smart Hall

PROMOTIONS
Managing Editors: Tena Kelley Vaughn and Marjorie Ann Lacy
Associate Editors: Steven M. Cooper, Dixie L. Morris,
 and Jennifer Leigh Ertl
Designer: Dale Rowett
Art Director: Linda Lovette Smart
Production Artist: Leslie Loring Krebs
Publishing Systems Administrator: Cindy Lumpkin
Publishing Systems Assistant: Susan Mary Gray

BUSINESS STAFF

Publisher: Bruce Akin
Vice President, Marketing: Guy A. Crossley
Marketing Manager: Byron L. Taylor
Print Production Manager: Laura Lockhart
Vice President and General Manager: Thomas L. Carlisle
Retail Sales Director: Richard Tignor

Vice President, Retail Marketing: Pam Stebbins
Retail Marketing Director: Margaret Sweetin
Retail Customer Services Manager: Carolyn Pruss
General Merchandise Manager: Russ Barnett
Vice President, Finance: Tom Siebenmorgen
Distribution Director: Ed M. Strackbein

Library of Congress Catalog Number 96-78948
International Standard Book Number 0-8487-4159-5

CHRISTMAS GIFTS of GOOD TASTE

*D*elighting those we love with the perfect present is a treasured Christmas tradition. And each offering is even more meaningful when we've taken the time to make, bake, and create it at home. With this in mind, Leisure Arts is happy to present Christmas Gifts of Good Taste as your creative guide to holiday giving! From cover to cover, there's a sleighload of delicious foods and charming crafts developed especially for Yuletide celebrations. We even have yummy treats prepared with secret recipes from Santa's sweetshop! But most importantly, you'll find unique gift ideas that allow you to deliver tailor-made presents to everyone on your list. So spend a few evenings in the kitchen and a little time in your craft room, and let all of your seasonal sharing reflect a simple message: "This gift was created especially for you with my hands, as well as my heart."

Anne Childs

LEISURE ARTS, INC.
Little Rock, Arkansas

Table of Contents

SPICED HONEY

*I*f the holidays keep you busy as a bee, then you'll surely appreciate the ease of creating this sweet offering. Delectable Spiced Honey is ideal for anyone on your gift list, and it's prepared using only three ingredients. The simple basket, trimmed with festive ribbon and a tiny bee, makes a charming presentation for the jar of honey. For fun, include a honey wand and a "beary" special Christmas angel.

SPICED HONEY

  4 cups honey
  ¹/₂ teaspoon ground cloves
  4 cinnamon sticks

Combine honey and cloves in a medium saucepan. Add cinnamon sticks and heat over medium-high heat about 4 minutes or until very warm. Transfer 1 cinnamon stick to each of 4 half-pint jars. Fill with spiced honey. Cover and let stand 24 hours. Use spiced honey to sweeten tea and on breads. Store at room temperature up to 3 weeks.

Yield: about 4 cups spiced honey

LEMON-GINGER LIQUEUR

Lemon-Ginger Liqueur is a delightful Christmas cordial that promises to brighten holiday spirits! Presented in a decorative decanter, the sweetened beverage can be served as a wonderful completion to a Yuletide dinner.

LEMON-GINGER LIQUEUR

- 4 lemons
- 1 bottle (750 ml) vodka
- 1/4 teaspoon ground ginger
- 1 1/2 cups superfine sugar

Peel zest (yellow portion) from lemons. Combine vodka, lemon zest, and ginger in a 1-quart airtight container. Let stand in a cool place 24 hours. Strain and discard lemon peel from vodka. Add sugar to vodka; stir until sugar dissolves. Let stand 1 month. Pour into a gift container.

Yield: about 4 cups liqueur

LUSCIOUS ORANGE-NUT BARS

*N*o one will guess how easy it is to make this elegant gift! Orange-Nut Bars have a buttery pecan crust topped with a fluffy fruit-flavored filling. As a hint to the luscious treats inside, the purchased gift box is decorated with fruit-inspired ribbon, a dried orange slice, and pecans.

ORANGE-NUT BARS

CRUST

- 1¹/₂ cups all-purpose flour
- ¹/₂ cup sifted confectioners sugar
- ²/₃ cup chopped pecans, toasted and coarsely ground
- ³/₄ cup butter or margarine, chilled

FILLING

- 1³/₄ cups sugar
- 4 eggs
- ¹/₃ cup orange juice
- ¹/₂ teaspoon orange extract
- ¹/₄ cup all-purpose flour
- ¹/₄ teaspoon baking powder

Preheat oven to 350 degrees. For crust, combine flour, confectioners sugar, and pecans in a medium bowl. Using a pastry blender or 2 knives, cut in butter until well blended. With lightly greased hands, press crust into bottom and ¹/₄ inch up sides of a greased 9 x 13-inch baking pan. Bake 20 minutes.

For filling, combine sugar, eggs, orange juice, and orange extract in a medium bowl; whisk until well blended. In a small bowl, combine flour and baking powder. Add dry ingredients to sugar mixture; whisk until well blended. Pour mixture over warm crust. Return to oven and bake 25 to 30 minutes longer or until filling is set. Cool in pan on a wire rack. Cut into 1 x 2-inch bars. Store in a single layer in an airtight container in refrigerator.

Yield: about 4 dozen bars

FESTIVE CHRISTMAS BRIE

*T*omato-Basil-Walnut Brie
*is sure to be warmly received
when you take it to a holiday
dinner party. Enfolded with
fresh basil leaves before baking,
the buttery-soft cheese is
complemented by a savory
sweetened tomato filling. Nestled
in a simply adorned basket, this
elegant appetizer is ready to go
to any Christmas gathering!*

TOMATO-BASIL-WALNUT BRIE

  1 can (6 ounces) tomato paste
  2 tablespoons firmly packed brown
      sugar
  2 tablespoons chopped fresh basil
      leaves
$^1/_2$ cup finely chopped walnuts, toasted
  1 package (8 ounces) round Brie
      cheese
  8 large whole fresh basil leaves

In a small bowl, combine tomato paste, brown sugar, and chopped basil leaves; stir until well blended. Stir in walnuts. Place whole basil leaves in a circle in a round 2-cup oven-proof dish. Slice off top one-third of cheese. Place bottom two-thirds of cheese on leaves. Spoon about $^1/_2$ cup tomato mixture onto cheese. Top with remaining piece of cheese. Spread remaining tomato mixture over top of cheese. Fold basil leaves over tomato mixture. Cover and store in refrigerator. Give with serving instructions.

Yield: 2 cups spread, 10 to 12 servings

To serve: Bake appetizer in a 350-degree oven 35 minutes or until cheese melts.

Tomato-Basil-Walnut
Brie
Bake 35 minutes at
350 degrees
or until cheese melts.

GINGERBREAD COOKIE ROUNDS

*O*ur cheerfully decorated Gingerbread Cookie Rounds combine traditional Christmas flavor with a hint of mocha. A fitting gift from one family to another, the spicy cookies are delivered in a sweetly embellished gingerbread box. The colorful container is covered with fused-on fabric and topped with swirls and dots of dimensional paint. A matching gift tag completes your surprise.

GINGERBREAD COOKIE ROUNDS

COOKIES

- 1/2 cup butter or margarine, softened
- 1/2 cup firmly packed brown sugar
- 1/2 cup granulated sugar
- 1/2 cup molasses
- 1/4 cup strongly brewed coffee
- 1 egg
- 1 teaspoon vanilla extract
- 3 cups all-purpose flour
- 1/4 cup cocoa
- 1 1/2 teaspoons ground ginger
- 1 teaspoon ground cinnamon
- 1 teaspoon baking soda
- 1/4 teaspoon ground cloves
- 1/4 teaspoon salt

ICING

- 1/2 cup sifted confectioners sugar
- 1 tablespoon vegetable shortening
- 1 tablespoon butter or margarine, softened
- 1 to 2 teaspoons water
- 1/4 teaspoon vanilla extract

For cookies, cream butter and sugars in a large bowl until fluffy. Add molasses, coffee, egg, and vanilla; beat until smooth. In a medium bowl, combine flour, cocoa, ginger, cinnamon, baking soda, cloves, and salt. Add dry ingredients to creamed mixture; stir until a soft dough forms. Cover and chill 1 hour.

Preheat oven to 350 degrees. On a lightly floured surface, use a floured rolling pin to roll out dough to 1/8-inch thickness. Use a floured 3-inch-diameter fluted-edge cookie cutter to cut out cookies. Transfer to a greased baking sheet. Bake 6 to 8 minutes or until bottoms are lightly browned. Transfer to a wire rack to cool completely.

For icing, beat confectioners sugar, shortening, butter, water, and vanilla in a small bowl until smooth. Spoon icing into a pastry bag fitted with a small round tip. Pipe decorations onto cookies. Let icing harden. Store in an airtight container.

Yield: about 3 1/2 dozen cookies

"GINGERBREAD" BOX

You will need a 6"w hexagon-shaped papier-mâché box; fabric to cover box; fusible web; white, red, and green dimensional paint; brown acrylic paint; paintbrush; 1 yd each of 3 different narrow ribbons; tracing paper; graphite transfer paper; glue; and colored paper and a gift label for tag.

1. Remove lid from box. To cover sides of box, fuse web to wrong side of fabric. Measure height of box; add 1/2". Measure around box; add 1". Cut a fabric strip the determined measurements.

2. Press 1 end of fabric strip 1/2" to wrong side. Beginning with unpressed end and matching 1 long edge of strip to top edge of box, fuse fabric strip around box. Glue fabric at overlap to secure. At bottom of box, clip fabric at each corner to about 1/8" from bottom of box. Fuse clipped edges of fabric to bottom of box.

3. To cover bottom of box, use a pencil to draw around bottom of box on fabric. Cut out fabric shape about 1/8" inside drawn lines. Center and fuse fabric shape to bottom of box.

4. For lid, paint lid brown. Trace pattern, page 112, onto tracing paper. Use transfer paper to transfer pattern to center top of lid.

5. Use white paint to paint over lines and dots indicated in grey on pattern. Use red and green paint to paint remaining dots as indicated on pattern.

6. Place gift in box and replace lid. Tie ribbons together into a bow around box; trim ends. If using curling ribbon, curl ends.

7. For tag, apply label to paper piece. Cutting around label, cut tag shape from paper. Write greeting on tag. Tuck tag under ribbons on box.

AMARETTO TRUFFLES

*M*iniature gift box
ornaments are just the right
size for sharing our heavenly
Amaretto Truffles. Incredibly
rich and smooth, the divine
little bites offer triple almond
flavor, including amaretto,
almond extract, and a toasted
almond coating.*

AMARETTO TRUFFLES

- 2/3 cup whipping cream
- 1 package (8 ounces) semisweet
    baking chocolate, finely chopped
- 2 cups slivered almonds, toasted,
    finely chopped, and divided
- 3 tablespoons amaretto
- 1 teaspoon almond extract

In a small saucepan, bring whipping
cream to a boil over medium-low heat.
Remove from heat. Add chocolate; stir
until chocolate melts. Transfer to a
medium bowl. Stir in 1 cup almonds,
amaretto, and almond extract. Cool
30 minutes; cover and chill 2 hours.

Drop rounded teaspoonfuls of
chocolate mixture onto a baking sheet
lined with waxed paper. Chill 30 minutes
in freezer or 2 hours in refrigerator.

Process remaining 1 cup almonds in a
food processor until coarsely ground.
Shape chilled chocolate mixture into
1-inch balls; roll in ground almonds.
Store in an airtight container in
refrigerator.

Yield: about 3 1/2 dozen truffles

FABULOUS FOUR CHIPS FUDGE

*W*hat sweeter way to offer happy holiday greetings than with gifts of fabulous Four Chips Fudge! The nut-filled confection is created with semisweet chocolate, milk chocolate, peanut butter, and butterscotch chips. For a presentation with flair, the rich, creamy bites are packed in ribbon-tied gold boxes.

FOUR CHIPS FUDGE

- 3/4 cup butter or margarine
- 1 can (14 ounces) sweetened condensed milk
- 3 tablespoons milk
- 1 package (12 ounces) semisweet chocolate chips
- 1 package (11¹/₂ ounces) milk chocolate chips
- 1 package (10 ounces) peanut butter chips
- 1 cup butterscotch chips
- 1 jar (7 ounces) marshmallow creme
- 1¹/₂ teaspoons vanilla extract
- 1 teaspoon almond extract
- 4 cups coarsely chopped walnuts

Line a 10¹/₂ x 15¹/₂-inch jellyroll pan with aluminum foil, extending foil over ends of pan; grease foil. Melt butter in a heavy Dutch oven over low heat; stir in sweetened condensed milk and milk. Add semisweet, milk chocolate, peanut butter, and butterscotch chips; stir until smooth. Remove from heat; stir in marshmallow creme and extracts. Stir in walnuts. Spread mixture into prepared pan. Chill 1 hour.

Use ends of foil to lift fudge from pan. Cut into 1-inch pieces. Store in an airtight container in refrigerator.

Yield: about 12 dozen pieces fudge

ROSEMARY CHICKEN-POTATO SALAD

When the holidays roll around, lend a helping hand to a busy friend with this all-in-one meal! Rosemary Chicken-Potato Salad features tender potatoes and chicken tossed in a zesty dressing along with fresh herbs and vegetables. It's perfect for lunch on a hectic day! Share our charming country Christmas towel along with the filling dish, and memories of your thoughtfulness will be rekindled throughout the season.

$\frac{1}{4}$ cup chicken broth
4 tablespoons freshly squeezed lemon juice, divided
3 tablespoons honey
2 tablespoons coarsely chopped fresh rosemary
1 clove garlic, minced
$1\frac{1}{2}$ teaspoons salt, divided
$\frac{1}{4}$ plus $\frac{1}{8}$ teaspoon ground black pepper, divided
$1\frac{1}{4}$ pounds boneless, skinless chicken breasts
2 pounds red potatoes, peeled and cubed
1 cup mayonnaise
$\frac{1}{2}$ cup finely chopped celery
$\frac{1}{4}$ cup finely chopped green onions
$\frac{1}{4}$ cup chopped sweet red pepper
1 tablespoon finely chopped fresh parsley
$\frac{1}{2}$ teaspoon grated lemon zest

In a medium bowl, combine chicken broth, 3 tablespoons lemon juice, honey, rosemary, garlic, $\frac{1}{4}$ teaspoon salt, and $\frac{1}{8}$ teaspoon black pepper. Place chicken in marinade, turning to coat well. Cover and chill 30 minutes.

Place potatoes in a heavy medium saucepan. Add water to cover potatoes. Add $\frac{3}{4}$ teaspoon salt. Cover and cook over medium-high heat about 15 minutes or just until tender. Drain and cool.

Place chicken and marinade in a medium skillet. Cover and cook over medium-low heat 25 to 30 minutes, turning once halfway through cooking time. Discard liquid and cool chicken slightly; cut into about $\frac{1}{2}$-inch pieces. In a large bowl, combine chicken and potatoes.

In a medium bowl, combine mayonnaise, celery, green onions, red pepper, parsley, remaining 1 tablespoon lemon juice, lemon zest, remaining $\frac{1}{2}$ teaspoon salt, and remaining $\frac{1}{4}$ teaspoon black pepper. Add dressing to chicken mixture; gently toss until coated. Cover and store in refrigerator.

Yield: about 8 cups salad

COUNTRY CHRISTMAS TOWEL

You will need a kitchen towel, fabrics for appliqué background and appliqués, fusible web, clear nylon thread and thread to match towel, embroidery floss to match fabrics, and 1 large and 2 small buttons.

1. Fuse web to wrong sides of background fabrics.
2. Measure width of towel. Cut a strip from 1 background fabric 4"w by the determined measurement. Cut a strip from remaining background fabric $2\frac{3}{4}$"w by the determined measurement.
3. Fuse wide strip about $2\frac{1}{2}$" from 1 end (bottom) of towel. Center and fuse narrow strip on wide strip.
4. Thread machine with clear thread and use thread to match towel in bobbin. Using a medium-width zigzag stitch with a medium stitch length, stitch over edges of background strips.
5. Use patterns, page 113, and follow *Making Appliqués*, page 121, to make 2 chickens (1 in reverse) and 1 of each star from fabrics.
6. Arrange appliqués on background fabric strips; fuse in place.
7. Repeat Step 4 to stitch over edges of appliqués.
8. Use floss to sew small buttons to chickens for eyes. Sew large button to center of stars and tie ends of floss into a bow at front; trim ends.

SANTA'S YUM-YUM BARS

*R*eward friends who've been especially sweet with yummy Candy Bar Fudge. Easily prepared in the microwave, the dreamy confection layers buttery fudge, nut-filled caramel, and chocolate candy coating. Individual bars are covered with foil and presented in cheery hand-colored wrappers.

CANDY BAR FUDGE

  1 cup butter or margarine, cut into pieces
  ¹/₃ cup cocoa
  3 cups sifted confectioners sugar
  1 package (14 ounces) caramels
  ¹/₄ cup milk
  2 cups lightly salted peanuts
  ¹/₂ cup milk chocolate chips
  4 ounces chocolate candy coating, cut into pieces

Line a 9 x 13-inch baking pan with aluminum foil, extending foil over ends of pan; grease foil. Place butter and cocoa in a medium microwave-safe bowl. Microwave on high power (100%) 1 minute or until butter melts; stir until smooth. Beat in confectioners sugar until well blended. Spread mixture into prepared pan. In a small microwave-safe bowl, combine caramels and milk. Microwave on high power (100%) 3 minutes or until smooth, stirring after each minute. Stir in peanuts. Spread caramel mixture over chocolate mixture.

In a small microwave-safe bowl, combine chocolate chips and candy coating. Microwave on medium-high power (80%) 2 minutes or until chocolate softens; stir until smooth. Spread chocolate over caramel layer. Cover and chill 2 hours or until chocolate hardens.

Cut into 1¹/₂ x 4-inch bars. Wrap individual bars in aluminum foil. Store in refrigerator.

Yield: about 16 bars

SANTA WRAPPER

You will need a photocopy of label design (page 113), a 3³/₄" x 5" piece of red paper, colored pencils, and glue.

1. Use pencils to color photocopy of label design. Cutting close to design, cut out label.
2. For wrapper, glue label across center of red paper.
3. Wrap wrapper around candy bar and glue to secure.

CHRISTMAS ICE-CREAM PARTY

*D*uring the busy
holidays, why not get together
with friends for a casual ice-
cream party! Catching up on
the latest news will be more
fun over frosty treats served
in nutty chocolate-dipped
sugar cones! For a great
conversation starter, a crafty
basket is filled with the
tasty cones and a handy
ice-cream dipper.

FUN SUGAR CONES

  3 ounces chocolate candy coating
$1/2$ cup semisweet chocolate chips
  1 package ($4^1/2$ ounces) sugar
      ice-cream cones
$3/4$ cup chopped pecans, toasted and
      coarsely ground

Combine candy coating and chocolate
chips in a small saucepan. Stirring
frequently, melt chocolate over low heat.
Remove from heat (if chocolate begins to
harden, return to heat). Dip about 1 inch
of top of each cone into melted chocolate,
allowing excess chocolate to drip back
into pan. Dip cones into pecans, lightly
pressing pecans into chocolate. Place
cones on a baking sheet lined with waxed
paper. Chill 30 minutes or until chocolate
hardens. Store in an airtight container in
refrigerator.

Yield: 12 cones

"here's the scoop..."
HAPPY HOLIDAYS!

TEACHER'S BROWNIES

*H*ow do you create an A⁺ gift for a teacher?
It's elementary, my dear! Simply stir up a batch of
Blackboard Brownies (made using a prepared mix),
decorate them with icing, and then place the chewy
squares in a novel fabric-covered "book" box.
The teacher will think you're one smart cookie!

BLACKBOARD BROWNIES

BROWNIES

- 1 package (22 ounces) brownie mix with walnuts
- 1/3 cup vegetable oil
- 1/3 cup water
- 1 egg
- 4 1/2 ounces white baking chocolate, coarsely chopped

CHOCOLATE ICING

- 1 cup semisweet chocolate chips
- 1/4 cup whipping cream
- 2 tablespoons butter or margarine
- 1/2 cup sifted confectioners sugar

WHITE CHOCOLATE ICING

- 1 1/2 ounces white baking chocolate

Preheat oven to 350 degrees. Line a 9 x 13-inch baking pan with aluminum foil, extending foil over ends of pan; grease foil. For brownies, combine brownie mix, oil, water, and egg in a large bowl; stir until blended. Stir white baking chocolate into brownie mixture. Spread batter into prepared pan. Bake 22 to 25 minutes. Cool in pan on a wire rack. Invert brownies onto a flat surface; remove foil.

For chocolate icing, combine chocolate chips, whipping cream, and butter in top of a double boiler over hot water. Whisking frequently, cook about 5 minutes or until chocolate melts and mixture is smooth. Remove from heat; whisk in confectioners sugar. Spread icing on brownies. Allow icing to cool. Cut brownies into 2-inch squares.

For white chocolate icing, melt white baking chocolate in a small saucepan over low heat, stirring constantly. Spoon chocolate into a pastry bag fitted with a very small tip. Pipe chocolate onto brownies to decorate. Allow chocolate to harden. Store in an airtight container.

Yield: about 2 dozen brownies

A BOOK FOR TEACHER

You will need a 7" x 9" papier-mâché "book" box; three coordinating fabrics to cover outside, inside, and spine and corners of book; 2/3 yd of 5/8"w "ruler" ribbon; large button and embroidery floss to coordinate with fabrics; spray adhesive; small scissors; and glue.

1. (*Note:* Throughout these instructions, we refer to the book box as "book.") Cut the following fabric pieces to cover book:

   11" x 17 1/2" for outside
   4" x 11" for spine
   2" square cut diagonally for corners
   2 5/8" x 21 1/4" for "pages"
   2" x 21" for inside of "pages"
   8 1/4" x 14 1/2" for remaining lining

2. (*Note:* Apply spray adhesive to wrong sides of all fabric pieces before applying to book.) To cover outside of book, center book on fabric piece and press fabric around book. Fold corners of fabric diagonally over corners onto sides of book; press edges of fabric over edges onto sides of book.

3. For spine, center spine of book on fabric piece (Fig. 1). Press fabric in place around book. Press excess fabric over edges of book at top and bottom.

Fig. 1

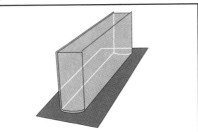

4. For corners, press triangles onto front of book with edges extending about 1/2" beyond edges of book (Fig. 2). Press excess fabric around corners of book.

Fig. 2

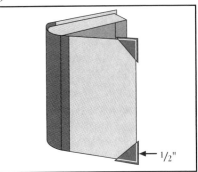

5. To cover "pages," match 1 long edge of fabric to bottom edge of "pages" and press fabric strip onto "pages." Use small scissors to trim ends of fabric strip to fit curved spine of book. Wrap excess fabric to inside of book.

6. For lining, press fabric strip for inside of "pages" onto inside of "pages" of book. Press remaining fabric piece onto inside of lid, spine, and bottom of book (Fig. 3).

Fig. 3

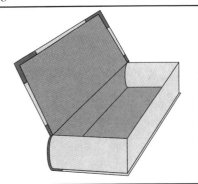

7. For closure, cut ribbon in half. Glue 1 end of 1 ribbon length to opening edge of front of book; glue 1 end of remaining length to back of book. Trim ribbon ends. Thread embroidery floss through button; knot and trim ends at back. Glue button over ribbon end on front of book. Tie ribbons into a bow.

HOT AND SPICY MUSTARD

Spread holiday cheer with a gift of Hot and Spicy Mustard. A saucy condiment for pretzels, the peppery spread is created simply by blending spices with prepared mustard. For a merry Christmas touch, present the mustard with a quick-and-easy cross-stitched elf ornament.

HOT AND SPICY MUSTARD

 1 jar (9 ounces) prepared mustard
 $^1/_2$ teaspoon crushed red pepper flakes
 2 cloves garlic, minced
 $^1/_4$ teaspoon ground allspice

Combine all ingredients in a medium bowl. Store in an airtight container in refrigerator at least 2 days to let flavors blend.

Yield: about 1 cup mustard

ELF ORNAMENT

You will need a 5" square of Antique White Aida (14 ct), embroidery floss (see color key, page 113), a 5" square of felt for backing, a 2$^1/_2$" dia. red Flexi-hoop™ embroidery frame, a chalk pencil, and glue.

1. Center and stitch elf design, page 113, on Aida, using 3 strands of floss for Cross Stitch and 1 strand for Backstitch.

2. For backing, use chalk pencil to draw around inner ring of frame on felt. Cut out circle. Center stitched piece in frame and replace inner ring. Trim edges of stitched piece close to inner ring. Glue backing over back of ornament.

DIXIE RELISH

*D*uring the fast-paced holidays, eating on the run doesn't have to be boring! A simple hot dog topped with sweet, tangy Dixie Relish is a wonderful way to wake up your taste buds. The colorful condiment combines cabbage, red and green peppers, and apple cider vinegar. For gift giving, pack jars of relish in tissue-lined foam containers. Assorted felt-tip pens are used to color the fun labels.

DIXIE RELISH

- 4 cups chopped green cabbage
- 2 cups chopped onions
- 2 cups chopped green peppers
- 2 cups chopped sweet red peppers
- $^{1}/_{2}$ cup salt
- 2 quarts water
- 2 cups apple cider vinegar
- 1 cup water
- $^{3}/_{4}$ cup sugar
- 2 tablespoons mustard seed
- 2 tablespoons celery seed
- $^{1}/_{2}$ teaspoon dried crushed red pepper flakes

In a large non-aluminum container, combine cabbage, onions, green peppers, and red peppers; toss well. Sprinkle with salt. Add 2 quarts water; cover and let stand 1 hour. Drain well. Rinse with cold water and drain again.

In a large Dutch oven over medium-high heat, combine vegetable mixture, vinegar, 1 cup water, sugar, mustard seed, celery seed, and red pepper flakes. Bring to a boil. Reduce heat to medium-low. Stirring occasionally, simmer uncovered 20 minutes. Spoon relish into heat-resistant jars. Cover with lids and cool. Store in refrigerator.

Yield: about 8$^{3}/_{4}$ cups relish

RELISH CONTAINER

For each container, you will need a 3$^{1}/_{2}$" x 7" take-out container, construction paper, tissue paper, black and assorted colors of felt-tip pens, serrated-cut craft scissors, tracing paper, graphite transfer paper, curling ribbon, and glue.

1. For label, use serrated-cut craft scissors to cut an approx. 1$^{3}/_{4}$" x 4$^{1}/_{2}$" piece of construction paper to fit on lid of container. Trace "Dixie Relish" pattern, page 114, onto tracing paper. Use transfer paper to transfer design to construction paper piece. Use pens to color design. Glue label to top of container.
2. Use craft scissors to cut a piece of tissue paper to line container. Place tissue paper in container and lay jar on paper.
3. Cut 2 lengths of curling ribbon. Glue center of ribbon lengths to closure tab on container bottom. Insert 1 end of ribbons through hole in tab on container top. Tie ribbons into a bow; curl ends.

CINNAMON-PRALINE PECANS

*R*ich nuggets of sweet delight, Cinnamon-Praline Pecans are baked in a flavorful coating of brown sugar, praline liqueur, and cinnamon. Tucked inside a ready-made wire stocking, the irresistible tidbits make a sophisticated gift.

CINNAMON-PRALINE PECANS

1 egg white
$^1/_2$ cup firmly packed brown sugar
1 tablespoon praline liqueur
1 teaspoon ground cinnamon
$^1/_2$ teaspoon vanilla extract
$^1/_2$ teaspoon butter extract
$^1/_8$ teaspoon salt
2 cups pecan halves

Preheat oven to 225 degrees. In a medium bowl, beat egg white until soft peaks form. Fold in brown sugar, liqueur, cinnamon, extracts, and salt. Fold in pecans. Bake 1 hour in a single layer on a greased nonstick $10^1/_2$ x $15^1/_2$-inch jellyroll pan. Spread on aluminum foil to cool. Store in an airtight container.

Yield: about 4 cups pecans

HEAVENLY CHERRY SAUCE

*F*riends who love ice-cream treats will adore the zippy taste of Very Cherry Sauce, a sassy combination of maraschino cherries and cherry preserves. Deliver this heavenly concoction in a gilded gift bag embellished with angel stickers, shiny ribbon, and an iridescent bow.

VERY CHERRY SAUCE

  1 jar (10 ounces) maraschino cherries
  1 jar (18 ounces) cherry preserves

Process undrained maraschino cherries in a food processor until coarsely chopped. Combine cherries and cherry preserves in a medium saucepan. Stirring frequently, cook mixture over medium heat about 5 minutes or until preserves melt. Store in an airtight container in refrigerator. Serve cold over ice cream or pound cake.

Yield: about 2²/₃ cups cherry sauce

HEAVENLY BAG

You will need a white lunch bag, ²/₃ yd of 1³/₈"w wired white ribbon, gold curling ribbon, angel stickers, gold acrylic paint, natural sponge piece, stapler, and glue.

1. Using gold paint and sponge piece, follow *Sponge Painting*, page 121, to paint bag.

2. Place gift in bag. Fold top of bag about 1" to front; fold 1" to front again and staple at center to secure.
3. Tie white ribbon into a bow; trim ends. Glue bow to bag over staple.
4. Tie several lengths of curling ribbon into bows and glue to bow on bag; curl ends. Apply stickers to bow and bag.

23

ZESTY CRAB SPREAD

*B*ring a taste of summer fun to the holidays with piquant Baked Crab Spread. Spiced with horseradish and hot pepper sauce, this savory appetizer is delicious with crackers. Wrap the dish in clear cellophane and tie on a cute seashell wreath to please a beachcombing friend. Don't forget the serving instructions!

BAKED CRAB SPREAD

  1 package (8 ounces) cream cheese, softened
$^1/_2$ cup mayonnaise
  2 tablespoons freshly squeezed lemon juice
  1 tablespoon grated onion
  1 tablespoon prepared horseradish
$^1/_4$ teaspoon garlic salt
$^1/_4$ teaspoon ground white pepper
$^1/_8$ teaspoon hot pepper sauce
  8 ounces fresh crabmeat *or* 2 cans crabmeat (6 ounces each), drained
$^1/_4$ cup finely chopped water chestnuts

In a large bowl, beat cream cheese, mayonnaise, lemon juice, onion, horseradish, garlic salt, white pepper, and pepper sauce until well blended. Fold in crabmeat and water chestnuts. Spoon into a 3-cup baking dish. Cover and store in refrigerator. Give with serving instructions.

Yield: about 2$^1/_2$ cups spread

To serve: Uncover and bake in a 350-degree oven 25 to 30 minutes or until lightly browned around edges. Serve warm with crackers.

SEASHELL WREATH ORNAMENT

You will need a 4" square of foam core board, $^3/_4$ yd of $^1/_4$"w ribbon, seashells (available at craft stores), tracing paper, craft knife, cutting mat, and glue.

1. Trace wreath pattern, page 114, onto tracing paper; cut out. Draw around pattern on foam core board. Use craft knife to cut out wreath shape.

2. Glue seashells to wreath shape.
3. Cut two 11" lengths from ribbon. Tie ribbon lengths together into a bow; trim ends. Glue bow to top of wreath.
4. For hanger, glue ends of remaining ribbon length to top back of ornament.

CREAMY PEPPERMINT CANDY

*O*ur Old-fashioned
*Peppermint Candy is so creamy
and delicious, everyone will
think it was made in Santa's
sweetshop! During the holidays,
keep some candy and festive
bags on hand to make instant
gifts for unexpected guests.*

OLD-FASHIONED PEPPERMINT CANDY

- 4 cups sugar
- 1 cup water
- 2 tablespoons light corn syrup
- 1/8 teaspoon salt
- 1 cup whipping cream
- 6 drops peppermint-flavored oil
     (used in candy making)

Butter sides of a heavy 6-quart Dutch oven. Combine sugar, water, corn syrup, and salt in Dutch oven. Stirring constantly, cook over medium-low heat until sugar dissolves. Using a pastry brush dipped in hot water, wash down any sugar crystals on sides of pan. Attach a candy thermometer to pan, making sure thermometer does not touch bottom of pan. Increase heat to high and bring to a boil; boil 2 minutes. Reduce heat to medium. Without stirring, slowly add whipping cream. Cook, without stirring, until mixture reaches 260 degrees. Test about 1/2 teaspoon of mixture in ice water. Mixture will roll into a hard ball in ice water and will remain hard when removed from the water. Pour mixture onto a flat, buttered surface; add peppermint oil. Use a spatula to fold edges of candy back onto itself until cool enough to handle. Use greased hands to pull candy to about a 15-inch length. Fold candy back onto itself and continue pulling, folding, and twisting until candy holds its shape and turns white. Pull and twist into a long rope about 3/4 inch in diameter. Use kitchen scissors to cut into 3/4-inch-long pieces. Transfer candy pieces to waxed paper and allow to cool completely. Cover loosely with waxed paper and let stand overnight to develop a creamy texture.

Wrap candy pieces individually in waxed paper, if desired. Store in an airtight container.

Yield: about 2 pounds candy

FRIENDSHIP OFFERING

*W*hen everyone gets together for a holiday open house, treat the group to Friendship Fruit Upside-Down Cake. The enticing dessert is prepared with Friendship Fruit Sauce and features a nutty brown-sugar topping and spicy cake. Our decoupaged plate makes a lovely token for the hostess.

FRIENDSHIP FRUIT SAUCE

YEAST STARTER
  1 cup sugar
  2 packages dry yeast
  1 can (15$^1/4$ ounces) pineapple
      chunks in heavy syrup

FRUIT SAUCE
  1 recipe yeast starter
  1 can (15$^1/4$ ounces) pineapple
      chunks in heavy syrup
  4 cups sugar, divided
  1 can (16 ounces) sliced peaches in
      syrup
  1 can (14 ounces) apricot halves in
      syrup, cut in half
  1 jar (10 ounces) maraschino
      cherries, drained

For yeast starter, combine sugar, yeast, and undrained pineapple in a 1-quart nonmetal container with a loose-fitting lid. Stir several times during first day to make sure sugar and yeast dissolve. Let mixture stand 2 weeks at room temperature; stir daily.

For fruit sauce, place yeast starter in a 1-gallon nonmetal container with a loose-fitting lid. Add undrained pineapple and 1 cup of sugar. Let fruit mixture stand 1 week at room temperature; stir daily.

For week 2, add undrained peaches and 1 cup sugar; stir daily.

For week 3, add undrained apricot pieces and 1 cup sugar; stir daily.

For week 4, add drained cherries and remaining 1 cup sugar; stir daily.

At end of fourth week, let mixture stand 3 days longer at room temperature; stir daily. Fruit sauce is now ready to use. Serve over ice cream, pound cake, or use in Friendship Fruit Upside-Down Cake (recipe follows). Reserve at least 1$^1/2$ cups fruit sauce to start a new batch of sauce.

To replenish fruit sauce, add 1 can undrained fruit (alternating types of fruit) and 1 cup sugar for each $^2/3$ cup fruit and 1 cup syrup removed. Stir mixture daily. Remove at least $^2/3$ cup fruit and 1 cup syrup every 2 weeks and replenish.

Yield: about 10 cups fruit sauce

FRIENDSHIP FRUIT UPSIDE-DOWN CAKE

  2 tablespoons butter or margarine
 $^2/3$ cup drained fruit from Friendship
      Fruit Sauce
 $^1/4$ cup firmly packed brown sugar
 $^1/4$ cup chopped pecans
  1 cup all-purpose flour
 $^1/2$ cup granulated sugar
 $^1/2$ teaspoon baking powder
 $^1/2$ teaspoon ground cinnamon
 $^1/4$ teaspoon ground nutmeg
 $^1/4$ teaspoon salt
  1 cup syrup from Friendship Fruit
      Sauce
 2$^1/2$ tablespoons vegetable oil
  1 egg

Preheat oven to 350 degrees. Melt butter in an 8-inch-diameter cast-iron skillet. Stir in fruit, brown sugar, and pecans. In a medium bowl, combine flour, granulated sugar, baking powder, cinnamon, nutmeg, and salt. In a small bowl, combine syrup, oil, and egg; add to dry ingredients, stirring until well blended. Pour batter over brown sugar topping. Bake 35 to 40 minutes or until top is golden brown and a toothpick inserted in center of cake comes out clean. Cool in pan 5 minutes on a wire rack. Loosen edges of cake with a knife. Invert cake onto a serving plate. Serve warm.

Yield: about 8 servings

DECOUPAGED PLATE

You will need an approx. 10$^1/2$"w clear glass octagonal plate, an approx. 13" fabric square, matte Mod Podge® sealer, foam brush, and a craft knife.

1. Use foam brush to apply sealer evenly to bottom and edges of plate. With right side of fabric facing plate, center fabric square on bottom of plate and press in place. Working from center outward, gently smooth wrinkles or bubbles in fabric with brush.
2. When sealer is dry, carefully use craft knife to trim excess fabric even with edges of plate.
3. Apply 2 to 3 coats of sealer to bottom and edges of plate, covering edges of fabric.
4. Lightly hand wash plate after use.

SANGRIA JELLY

*S*hare this fruity Sangria Jelly with friends who enjoy gifts with spirit! Prepared with red wine, the flavorful jelly is easy to stir together. This gift is even more delightful when delivered in a spray-painted can that's lined with a torn-fabric square and decorated with matching fabric, greenery, and a painted wooden star.

SANGRIA JELLY

   3 cups sugar
1¹/₂ cups dry red wine
  ¹/₄ cup orange juice
   1 tablespoon grated orange zest
   2 teaspoons orange-flavored liqueur
   1 pouch (3 ounces) liquid fruit pectin

In a large Dutch oven, combine sugar, wine, orange juice, orange zest, and liqueur; stir until well blended. Stirring constantly over high heat, bring mixture to a rolling boil. Stir in liquid pectin. Stirring constantly, bring to a rolling boil again and boil 1 minute. Remove from heat; skim off foam. Spoon into heat-resistant jars; cover and cool to room temperature. Store in refrigerator.

Yield: about 4 cups jelly

CHRISTMAS CAN

You will need a can large enough to hold jelly jar, a torn fabric square to line can, 1" x 16" torn fabric strip, 1¹/₂"w wooden star cutout, small red button, short length of silk greenery garland, 15" of craft wire for handle, spray primer, red spray paint, wood-tone spray, yellow acrylic paint, paintbrush, black felt-tip pen, hammer and nail, scrap piece of wood, and glue.

1. Spray can with primer. Spray paint can red. Spray can lightly with wood-tone spray.

2. For handle, place can on wood piece and use hammer and nail to punch a hole in each side of can close to rim, punching holes from inside of can. Insert ends of wire length in holes; bend ends up and twist to secure.

3. Paint star yellow. Use pen to draw stitches along edges. Glue button to star.

4. Knot fabric strip around can. Bend greenery into a crescent shape. Glue greenery and star over knot.

5. Line can with fabric square.

HOLIDAY PRETZELS

A fun family gift, these easy-to-make Christmas Pretzels will bring holiday joy to young and old alike! The Bavarian-style treats are simply dipped in candy coating and sprinkled with colored decorating sugar for a sweet presentation. Our gift bag features a "peek-a-boo" window bordered with festive trims.

CHRISTMAS PRETZELS

1 tablespoon red coarse decorating sugar

1 tablespoon green coarse decorating sugar

1 tablespoon white coarse decorating sugar

18 ounces vanilla candy coating, cut into pieces

1 package (10 ounces) 3-inch-wide Bavarian-style pretzels

In a small bowl, combine red, green, and white decorating sugars. Stirring frequently, melt candy coating in a heavy medium saucepan over low heat. Remove from heat. Working with 6 pretzels at a time, dip each pretzel into candy coating. Transfer pretzels to waxed paper. Sprinkle pretzels with sugar mixture before coating hardens. Store in an airtight container in a cool place.

Yield: about 2 dozen pretzels

FESTIVE GIFT BAG

You will need a medium-size gift bag, ³/₄ yd each of 2 ribbons and 1 yd of a third ribbon for bow, 19" of

decorative braid, gold cord to replace bag handles (optional), 4 gold buttons, scrap paper, clear cellophane, craft knife and small cutting mat or folded newspaper, and glue.

1. For window in bag, cut a 3¹/₂" x 6" piece of scrap paper for pattern. Draw around pattern at center front of bag. Place cutting mat inside front of bag and use craft knife to cut out window along drawn lines.

2. Cut a piece of cellophane about 1" larger on all sides than window.

3. Center cellophane over window on inside of bag; glue in place.

4. Cut 9" from 1 yd ribbon length. Follow Step 1 of *Making a Multi-Loop Bow*, page 123, to make bow from remaining ribbon lengths; tie bow with 9" ribbon length at center to secure.

5. Glue braid along edges of window, buttons at corners, and bow at top.

6. If desired, remove handles from bag and replace with gold cord.

CHRISTMAS MORNING TREATS

*M*ake Christmas morning especially nice for a favorite couple with a gift of Pumpkin Bread and Cinnamon-Raisin Spread! A pound cake mix gives you a quick start to making the spicy nut-filled cake, and the creamy spread is prepared with only three ingredients. Offer your tasty surprises packed in a basket along with coffee mugs and a serving plate.

PUMPKIN BREAD AND CINNAMON-RAISIN SPREAD

SPREAD
- 2   containers (8 ounces each) soft cream cheese
- ¹/₂ cup golden raisins
- 1   teaspoon ground cinnamon

BREAD
- 1   package (16 ounces) pound cake mix
- 1   teaspoon pumpkin pie spice
- 1   teaspoon baking soda
- 1   cup canned pumpkin
- ¹/₂ cup orange juice
- 2   eggs
- 1   cup chopped walnuts

For spread, process cream cheese, raisins, and cinnamon in a food processor until raisins are coarsely chopped and mixture is well blended. Store in an airtight container in refrigerator 2 hours to let flavors blend.

Preheat oven to 325 degrees. For bread, grease bottoms of two 4¹/₂ x 8¹/₂-inch loaf pans and line bottoms with waxed paper. Grease and flour waxed paper and sides of pans. In a large bowl, combine cake mix, pumpkin pie spice, and baking soda. Add pumpkin, orange juice, and eggs; beat until well blended. Stir in walnuts. Spoon batter into prepared pans. Bake 42 to 46 minutes or until a toothpick inserted in center of bread comes out clean. Cool in pans 20 minutes. Remove from pans and serve warm or cool completely on a wire rack. Store in an airtight container.

Yield: 2 loaves bread and about 2 cups spread

"BERRY" EASY JAM

*S*hare the sweet flavor of raspberries with luscious Raspberry Refrigerator Jam. So much easier to make than traditional jams because it's meant to be stored in the fridge, this sweet spread is convenient to make with frozen raspberries and juice concentrate. As a special delivery for a gardener, a jar of jam is tucked inside a cloth-lined flowerpot painted with a berry motif. A matching tag helps to "spread" Christmas cheer!

RASPBERRY REFRIGERATOR JAM

1½ teaspoons unflavored gelatin
3 tablespoons frozen unsweetened grape juice concentrate, thawed
3 cups frozen raspberries
½ cup sugar

In a medium saucepan, sprinkle gelatin over grape juice concentrate; allow to stand 1 minute. Add raspberries and sugar. Stirring occasionally, cook over low heat until gelatin and sugar dissolve and berries are crushed. Spoon into jars; cover and cool to room temperature. Store in refrigerator.

Yield: about 2 cups jam

PAINTED FLOWERPOT AND JAR LID

You will need a 4¼"h clay flowerpot; a 10" torn fabric square; parchment paper; cream, pink, dark pink, dark red, green, dark green, and brown acrylic paint; foam brushes; small paintbrushes; toothpick; spray primer; tracing paper; graphite transfer paper; shredded paper to line pot; and paper, fabric, poster board, fusible web, and a black felt-tip pen for tag.

1. For flowerpot, spray pot with primer. Paint inside and rim of pot cream. Paint outside of pot below rim dark red.
2. For jar lid insert, use flat part of a jar lid (same size as jar lid used in storing food) as a pattern to cut a piece of parchment paper.
3. Trace patterns, page 114, separately onto tracing paper. Use graphite transfer paper to transfer designs to rim of pot and jar lid insert.
4. Paint large leaves green. Paint veins on leaves dark green. Paint small leaves green and dark green. Paint tendrils on jar lid insert green. Using handle end of paintbrush, use dark pink paint to paint clusters of dots for berries. Repeat to paint pink dots over dark pink dots. Use toothpick to paint cream dots for highlights on berries. Use brown paint to paint vine between leaves and berry clusters on pot.
5. Line pot with shredded paper. Place fabric square in pot. Place gift in pot.
6. For tag, follow *Making a Fabric-Backed Tag,* page 123. Use black pen to write message on tag.

CINNAMON APPLE BUTTER

*S*ay *"Merry Christmas"
to a favorite teacher with a
gift of homemade Cinnamon
Apple Butter. The sweet spread
is prepared with fresh apples,
brown sugar, and spices. For
an appealing presentation,
pack a jar of the butter and
some store-bought muffins in a
ready-made chalkboard basket.*

CINNAMON APPLE BUTTER

  6 pounds Rome or other cooking
     apples (about 12 apples),
     peeled, quartered, and cored
 1/3 cup water
1 1/2 cups firmly packed brown sugar
  1 cup apple cider
  2 tablespoons lemon juice
  2 teaspoons ground cinnamon
 1/4 teaspoon ground allspice
 1/4 teaspoon ground ginger

Combine apples and water in a Dutch
oven. Cover and cook over medium heat
about 20 minutes or until apples are soft.
Process apples in a food processor until
smooth. Combine cooked apples, brown
sugar, apple cider, lemon juice,
cinnamon, allspice, and ginger in Dutch
oven. Stirring frequently, cook uncovered
over low heat about 1 hour. Stirring
constantly, cook about 15 minutes longer
or until mixture thickens to desired
consistency. Store in an airtight container
in refrigerator.

Yield: about 8 cups apple butter

ORANGE-PECAN PIE

A homemade dessert is always an appropriate holiday gift, especially one as delectable as our Orange-Pecan Pie! A traditional Christmas sweet, this citrusy version is flavored with orange juice and orange zest. It's a snap to decorate the pie cover using festive wired ribbon and a pretty silk poinsettia.

ORANGE-PECAN PIE

- 3 eggs, beaten
- 1 cup dark corn syrup
- 1/2 cup sugar
- 1/3 cup orange juice
- 1 tablespoon grated orange zest
- 1 tablespoon all-purpose flour
- 1/4 teaspoon salt
- 1 cup chopped pecans
- 1 unbaked 9-inch pie crust
- 3/4 cup pecan halves

Preheat oven to 350 degrees. In a medium bowl, combine eggs, corn syrup, sugar, orange juice, orange zest, flour, and salt. Beat at medium speed of electric mixer until well blended. Stir in chopped pecans. Pour mixture into pie crust. Arrange pecan halves over top. Bake 55 to 60 minutes or until center is almost set. Transfer to a wire rack to cool. Store in an airtight container in refrigerator.

Yield: about 8 servings

MERRY "CHRIS-MOUSSE"!

*C*hocolate-Chocolate Mousse Pie is the natural gift choice for someone who appreciates the total satisfaction of chocolate! For an irresistible taste sensation, hints of mocha and almond are blended into the rich, airy filling, which is nestled in a buttery cookie crust. Easy to make using brown paper and a handcrafted moose stamp, the whimsical gift wrap and matching tag carry out your Merry "Chris-mousse" wishes!

CHOCOLATE-CHOCOLATE MOUSSE PIE

CRUST

    18 chocolate sandwich cookies
    1/4 cup chilled butter or margarine
     3 tablespoons sugar

FILLING

     1 tablespoon cocoa
    1/2 cup milk
    1/4 cup strongly brewed coffee
     3 eggs, separated
     8 ounces semisweet baking
        chocolate, cut into pieces
     1 teaspoon vanilla extract
    1/2 teaspoon almond extract
    1/3 cup sugar
     1 tablespoon water
    1/8 teaspoon cream of tartar
     1 cup whipping cream, whipped
        Chocolate curls to garnish

Preheat oven to 450 degrees. For crust, process cookies in a food processor until finely ground. Add butter and sugar; process until well blended. Press mixture into bottom and up sides of a 9-inch pie plate. Bake 6 minutes. Cool completely on a wire rack.

For filling, combine cocoa, milk, and coffee in top of a double boiler over simmering water; whisk until smooth. Whisk in egg yolks. Whisking constantly, cook 6 minutes or until mixture is thick enough to coat a spoon. Remove from heat. Add chocolate and extracts; stir until chocolate melts. Transfer chocolate mixture to a large bowl.

In top of a double boiler over simmering water, combine sugar, egg whites, water, and cream of tartar. Whisking constantly, cook mixture until a thermometer registers 160 degrees (about 10 minutes). Transfer to a medium bowl; beat until soft peaks form. Fold egg white mixture and whipped cream into chocolate mixture. Spoon mousse into crust. Cover and store in refrigerator. To serve, garnish with chocolate curls.

Yield: about 8 servings

MOOSE WRAPPING PAPER AND TAG

You will need brown wrapping paper, craft foam, a 4" square of heavy cardboard or foam core board, brown acrylic paint, paintbrush, black felt-tip pen, tracing paper, graphite transfer paper, jute twine, hole punch, and glue.

1. For stamp, trace moose pattern, page 114, onto tracing paper. Use transfer paper to transfer pattern to craft foam; cut out. Center and glue shape to cardboard.
2. Cut wrapping paper desired size.
3. For stamping guidelines, use a pencil and ruler to draw a line 3½" from top of paper. Draw a second line 1" below first line. Continue drawing lines at 3½" and 1" intervals to bottom of paper (Fig. 1).

Fig. 1

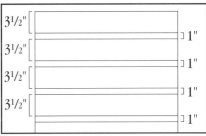

4. Use paintbrush to apply brown paint evenly to stamp. Press stamp on paper between lines spaced 3½" apart. Reapplying paint to stamp as necessary, repeat to stamp rows of moose on paper.
5. Use a pencil to write "Chocolate Mousse" on paper between lines spaced 1" apart. Use pen to draw over words.
6. For tag, cut a 3¾" x 7" piece of wrapping paper. Match short edges and fold in half. Repeat Step 4 to stamp moose on tag. Punch a hole in tag. Loop a length of twine through hole.

FESTIVE POPCORN

A plain white gift bag decorated with a flurry of painted snowflakes makes a cheery carrier for our sweet and crunchy Skater's Popcorn. The flavorful morsels are festively tinted with lime and cherry gelatin, then mixed with green and red jelly beans for holiday appeal. A purchased ornament tied to the bag will be a reminder of your thoughtfulness long after the snacks are gone.

SKATER'S POPCORN

Make 2 recipes of popcorn using different flavors of gelatin.

- 12 cups popped popcorn
- 6 tablespoons butter or margarine
- 3 cups miniature marshmallows
- 1/4 cup flavored gelatin (we used lime and cherry)
- 8 ounces small red gourmet jelly beans
- 8 ounces small green gourmet jelly beans

Preheat oven to 200 degrees. Place popcorn in a large roasting pan. In a medium microwave-safe bowl, microwave butter on high power (100%) 1 minute or until melted. Add marshmallows. Microwave 1 minute longer; stir until melted. Add gelatin; stir until gelatin dissolves. Pour gelatin mixture over popcorn; stir until well coated. Bake 40 minutes, stirring every 10 minutes. Cool completely. Stir in jelly beans. Store in an airtight container.

Yield: about 12 cups popcorn

ZESTY PINEAPPLE SPREAD

*D*uring the holiday snacking season, any calorie-conscious friend will be glad to receive our delicious Creamy Pineapple Spread! The reduced-fat topping is presented with fresh bagels in a fabric-lined gift basket.

CREAMY PINEAPPLE SPREAD

- 2 packages (8 ounces each) Neufchâtel cheese, softened
- 2 cans (8 ounces each) crushed pineapple, well drained
- 1 can (8 ounces) water chestnuts, drained and chopped
- 1/4 cup finely chopped green pepper
- 3 tablespoons finely chopped green onion
- 1 tablespoon prepared horseradish
- 1/2 teaspoon garlic salt
  Bagels to serve

In a medium bowl, beat cheese until fluffy. Stir in pineapple, water chestnuts, green pepper, green onion, horseradish, and garlic salt. Cover and chill overnight. Serve with bagels.

Yield: about 4 cups spread

"SQUARE-IN-A-SQUARE" GIFT BASKET

You will need fusible web and 5 different fabrics for appliqués.
For basket, you will *also* need a small basket and a fabric square for basket liner.
For container, you will *also* need a small acrylic container or jar with smooth flat

top, matte Mod Podge® sealer, a foam brush, and tracing paper.
For tag, you will *also* need a 2³/₄" x 5¹/₂" piece of desired color paper.

BASKET
1. Fringe edges of fabric square about ¹/₂".
2. Follow *Making Appliqués,* page 121, to make 4 appliqués for each of the 4 smallest squares in pattern, page 115.
3. Arrange appliqués on corners of fringed square; fuse in place.
4. Place liner in basket.

CONTAINER
1. Follow *Making Appliqués,* page 121, to make 1 appliqué for each of the 4 smallest squares in pattern, page 115.

2. Trace largest square in pattern onto tracing paper; cut out. Use pattern to cut large square from fabric. Arrange and fuse appliqués to large square.
3. Use sealer to glue design to lid of container.

TAG
1. Match short edges and fold paper piece in half.
2. Follow *Making Appliqués,* page 121, to make 1 appliqué for each square in pattern, page 115.
3. Arrange appliqués on tag and fuse in place.

'TIS THE "SEASON"!

T is the "season" to be jolly, so here are six savory blends to help you serve up Christmas cheer to several friends! Packaged individually in ribbon-tied cellophane bags, these flavor enhancers will bring out the natural goodness of seafood, poultry, vegetables, and much more. When sharing these gifts, be sure to include seasoning suggestions.

BAY SEAFOOD SEASONING

1   tablespoon crushed bay leaves
2¹/₂ teaspoons celery salt
1¹/₂ teaspoons dry mustard
1¹/₂ teaspoons ground black pepper
³/₄   teaspoon ground nutmeg
¹/₂   teaspoon ground cloves
¹/₂   teaspoon ground ginger
¹/₂   teaspoon paprika
¹/₂   teaspoon ground red pepper
¹/₄   teaspoon ground mace
¹/₄   teaspoon ground cardamom

Process all ingredients in a food processor until well blended. Store in an airtight container. Use seasoning with seafood or chicken.

Yield: about ¹/₄ cup seasoning

CREOLE SEASONING

1   tablespoon salt
1¹/₂ teaspoons garlic powder
1¹/₂ teaspoons onion powder
1¹/₂ teaspoons paprika
1¹/₄ teaspoons dried thyme leaves
1   teaspoon ground red pepper
³/₄   teaspoon ground black pepper
³/₄   teaspoon dried oregano leaves
¹/₂   teaspoon crushed bay leaf
¹/₄   teaspoon chili powder

Process all ingredients in a food processor until well blended. Store in an airtight container. Use seasoning with seafood, chicken, beef, or vegetables.

Yield: about ¹/₄ cup seasoning

GREEK SEASONING

2   teaspoons salt
2   teaspoons ground oregano
1¹/₂ teaspoons onion powder
1¹/₂ teaspoons garlic powder
1   teaspoon cornstarch
1   teaspoon ground black pepper
1   teaspoon beef bouillon granules
1   teaspoon dried parsley flakes
¹/₂   teaspoon ground cinnamon
¹/₂   teaspoon ground nutmeg

Process all ingredients in a food processor until well blended. Store in an airtight container. Use seasoning with steaks, pork chops, chicken, or fish.

Yield: about ¹/₄ cup seasoning

GROUND SEASONING

2   tablespoons celery seed
1   tablespoon onion powder
1   tablespoon salt

Process all ingredients in a food processor until well blended. Store in an airtight container. Use seasoning in stews, chowders, or sandwich spreads.

Yield: about ¹/₄ cup seasoning

FIVE-SPICE POWDER

2   teaspoons anise seeds, crushed
2   teaspoons ground black pepper
2   teaspoons fennel seeds, crushed
2   teaspoons ground cloves
2   teaspoons ground cinnamon
1¹/₂ teaspoons ground ginger
¹/₂   teaspoon ground allspice

Combine all ingredients; store in an airtight container. Use with fish or pork.

Yield: about ¹/₄ cup seasoning

HERBS SEASONING

1   tablespoon ground thyme
1   tablespoon dried oregano leaves
2   teaspoons rubbed sage
1   teaspoon dried rosemary leaves
1   teaspoon dried marjoram leaves
1   teaspoon dried basil leaves
1   teaspoon dried parsley flakes

Process all ingredients in a food processor until well blended. Store in an airtight container. Use seasoning in omelets or with fish, vegetables, or chicken.

Yield: about ¹/₄ cup seasoning

For each tag, follow *Making a Tag,* page 123.

SPICY WINTER WARMER

*S*pice up an offering of holiday spirits with our Hot Mulled Wine. The fruity drink is laced with cinnamon, cloves, and allspice for a flavorful winter warmer. Present a bottle of wine in a no-sew bag that's finished with a pretty bow and an ornament.

HOT MULLED WINE

2	quarts Burgundy or other dry red wine
2	quarts apple juice
3	cinnamon sticks (3 inches each)
1½	teaspoons whole cloves
1	teaspoon whole allspice

Combine wine and apple juice in a 1-gallon container. Tie spices in a small square of cheesecloth; add to wine mixture. Cover and chill overnight.

Remove spice bag and transfer wine to gift bottles. Store in refrigerator. Give with serving instructions.

Yield: about 4 quarts wine

To serve: Bring wine to a boil in a large Dutch oven. Reduce heat and simmer 3 to 5 minutes. Serve hot.

LUXURIOUS BOTTLE WRAP

You will need fabric, ½"w fusible web tape, ¾ yd of 2"w wired ribbon, 20" of cord, and an ornament.

1. Measure around bottle; divide by 2 and add 1½". Measure bottle from 1 side of top to opposite side of top (Fig. 1); add 8". Cut a piece of fabric the determined measurements.

Fig. 1

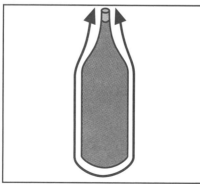

2. Matching right sides and short edges, press fabric piece in half (fold is bottom of bag). Unfold fabric piece and fuse web tape along each long edge on right side. Refold fabric piece and fuse edges together. Turn bag right side out. Fold top of bag 2½" to inside and press.
3. Place wine bottle in bag. Tie ribbon into a bow around bag; trim ends. Thread ornament onto cord and tie cord into a bow around bow on bag; knot ends.

SWEET & SPICY NUTS

*C*o-workers will be star-struck when they discover this celestial container of Sweet and Spicy Mixed Nuts! A crunchy treat for the whole bunch, the tangy mix is quick to stir up using a simple combination of spices. For a heavenly presentation, decorate a painted canister with golden stars and tuck a beribboned bag of the nutty snack inside.

SWEET AND SPICY MIXED NUTS

  1 tablespoon sugar
$1/2$ teaspoon ground cumin
$1/2$ teaspoon chili powder
$1/4$ teaspoon ground red pepper
$1/8$ teaspoon salt
  1 can (12 ounces) mixed nuts

Preheat oven to 325 degrees. In a medium bowl, combine sugar, cumin, chili powder, red pepper, and salt; set aside. Place nuts on a baking sheet. Bake 10 minutes. Toss warm nuts in spice mix until well coated. Transfer to baking sheet to cool. Store in an airtight container.

Yield: about $2^{1}/_{2}$ cups nuts

CELESTIAL CONTAINER

You will need an approx. $4^{1}/_{2}$"h galvanized tin container, dark red spray paint, metallic gold acrylic paint, small paintbrush, and a gold paint pen.

1. Spray paint container dark red.
2. Use paintbrush and gold paint to paint rim and bottom edge of container.
3. Use paint pen to paint stars and dots on container.

41

CHOCOLATE POUND CAKE

*L*et your holiday spirit shine by sharing our wonderful Chocolate Pound Cake with a neighbor who's homebound. A simple yet delicious variation of a traditional dessert, the cake is wonderfully moist and rich. Presented in a fabric-covered bag along with your warmest Yuletide wishes, this cake will make your friend feel like a star!

CHOCOLATE POUND CAKE

1½ cups butter or margarine, softened
2½ cups sugar
5 eggs
1 teaspoon vanilla
3 cups all-purpose flour
½ cup cocoa
½ teaspoon baking powder
½ teaspoon salt
1 cup milk

Preheat oven to 325 degrees. In a large bowl, cream butter and sugar until fluffy. Add eggs, 1 at a time, beating thoroughly after each addition. Stir in vanilla. In a medium bowl, combine flour, cocoa, baking powder, and salt. Alternately beat dry ingredients and milk into creamed mixture, beating until well blended. Pour batter into a greased 10-inch tube pan. Bake 1 hour 25 minutes or until a toothpick inserted in center of cake comes out clean. Cool in pan 15 minutes. Remove from pan and cool completely on a wire rack. Store in an airtight container.

Yield: about 16 servings

STARRY BAG

You will need a grocery bag, fabric, fusible web, 2½"w brown paper ribbon, assorted sizes of wooden star cutouts, yellow acrylic paint, paintbrush, black felt-tip pen, silk berry stem, floral wire, wire cutters, stapler, and glue.

1. Fuse web to wrong side of fabric.
2. Measure width of front of bag (Fig. 1); measure from center top of bag front to center back of bag bottom. Cut a piece of fabric the determined measurements. Fuse fabric piece to front and bottom of bag.

Fig. 1

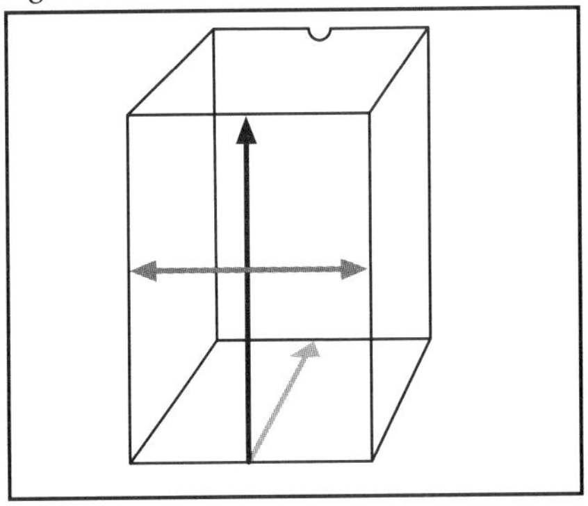

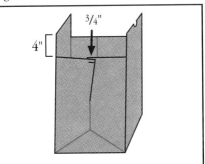

3. Cut away top 4" of each side of bag; staple a ³/₄" pleat in each side of bag (Fig. 2).

Fig. 2

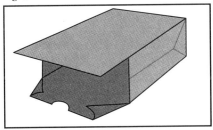

4. Place bag front side up. Fold corners of bottom flap diagonally toward center; glue to secure (Fig. 3). Fold bottom flap up and top flap down.

Fig. 3

5. Paint stars yellow. Use pen to draw details on stars.
6. Form a bow from paper ribbon; wrap with wire at center to secure. Trim ribbon ends.
7. Glue berry stem, bow, and stars to bag.

GOURMET ANTIPASTO

*T*he pleasing flavor of Marinated Artichokes and Mushrooms will delight friends who have gourmet tastes. Packed in a zesty seasoned marinade, the vegetables are a delicious accompaniment to pasta or chicken. You can complete this holiday treat by delivering jars of the antipasto in cute snowman watering cans. The carriers and matching gift tags are decorated with fabric motifs that are embellished with dimensional paints.

MARINATED ARTICHOKES AND MUSHROOMS

- 4 cans (14 ounces each) quartered artichokes, drained
- 1 package (8 ounces) fresh mushrooms, sliced
- 2 cups olive oil
- 3 tablespoons white wine vinegar
- 2½ tablespoons freshly squeezed lemon juice
- 4 cloves garlic, minced
- 2 teaspoons salt
- ¾ teaspoon dry mustard
- 2 tablespoons chopped fresh basil leaves

Combine artichokes and mushrooms in a large bowl. In a medium saucepan, combine oil, vinegar, lemon juice, garlic, salt, and dry mustard. Stirring frequently, bring mixture to a boil over medium-high heat. Remove from heat; stir in basil. Pour over artichoke mixture. Gently stir to coat vegetables. Store in an airtight container in refrigerator. Serve vegetables at room temperature.

Yield: about 8 cups marinated vegetables

SNOWMAN WATERING CAN

For each watering can, you will need a small galvanized watering can, snowman-motif fabric for appliqués, pinked fabric square to line can, dimensional paint to coordinate with fabrics, kraft paper, black felt-tip pen, jute twine, hole punch, serrated-cut craft scissors, and glue.

1. For tag, fold a piece of kraft paper in half and use craft scissors to trim edges. Punch hole in tag. Use black pen to draw a design around hole.
2. Cut motifs from fabric. Glue motifs to watering can and tag.
3. Use paint to outline and add details to motifs.
4. Use twine and follow Step 1 of *Making a Multi-Loop Bow*, page 123; tie bow with a length of twine at center to secure. Tie ends of same twine length around handle of watering can. Thread 1 end of twine through hole in tag; knot twine to secure.
5. Line can with fabric square.

SWEET JALAPEÑO SLICES

*F*or gifts that are guaranteed to warm up holiday meals, share jars of Sweet Jalapeño Pepper Slices. The fiery peppers add wonderful flavor to vegetables, sandwiches, and many other foods. Fabric jar covers and hand-colored, photocopied tags are easy embellishments for the jars.

SWEET JALAPEÑO PEPPER SLICES

For a milder taste, use mild jalapeño peppers.

- 1 gallon jalapeño pepper slices, drained
- 8 cloves garlic
- 6 cups sugar
- 4 cups apple cider vinegar
- 3 teaspoons celery seed
- 3 teaspoons mustard seed
- 1½ teaspoons ground turmeric

Place jalapeño pepper slices in 8 heat-resistant pint jars. Place 1 garlic clove in each jar. In a heavy Dutch oven, combine sugar, vinegar, celery seed, mustard seed, and turmeric. Stirring frequently, bring vinegar mixture to a boil over medium-high heat. Carefully pour hot vinegar mixture over jalapeño pepper slices. Allow mixture to cool. Cover with lids and chill 24 hours to let flavors blend. Store in refrigerator.

Yield: 8 pints jalapeño peppers

JAR COVERS AND GIFT TAGS

For each jar cover and tag, you will need an approx. 8" pinked fabric square, photocopy of desired tag design (page 123), paper to match fabric, colored pencils, felt-tip pen, jute twine, hole punch, and glue.

1. Use pencils to color photocopy of tag design. Use pen to personalize design.

2. Cut out tag and glue to colored paper. Cutting close to tag, cut tag from paper. Punch hole in tag.

3. Center fabric square on jar. Knot twine around fabric and jar. Thread tag onto 1 end of twine. Knot and trim ends of twine.

DELIGHTFUL LEMON CHEESECAKE

Wish someone a "Merry Christmas" with this tantalizing gift to complete a holiday dinner with style. Crowned with a smooth, tangy glaze and garnished with lemon peel curls, our creamy Lemon Cheesecake has a lively flavor. This delightful dessert is presented in an ordinary pie box decorated with wrapping paper, dimensional paint, and a shimmering ribbon bow.

LEMON CHEESECAKE

CRUST
- 2 cups graham cracker crumbs
- 1/4 cup plus 2 tablespoons butter or margarine, melted
- 2 tablespoons sugar

FILLING
- 3 packages (8 ounces each) cream cheese, softened
- 3/4 cup plus 3 tablespoons sugar, divided
- 3 eggs
- 1/4 cup freshly squeezed lemon juice
- 1 tablespoon grated lemon zest
- 3 teaspoons vanilla extract, divided
- 2 cups sour cream

LEMON GLAZE
- 1/2 cup sugar
- 1 1/2 tablespoons cornstarch
- 1/4 teaspoon salt
- 3/4 cup water
- 1/3 cup freshly squeezed lemon juice
- 1 egg yolk
- 1 tablespoon butter or margarine
- 1 1/2 teaspoons grated lemon zest
- 3 drops yellow food coloring
  Lemon peel curls to garnish

Preheat oven to 350 degrees. For crust, combine cracker crumbs, melted butter, and sugar in a medium bowl; stir until well blended. Press into bottom and halfway up sides of a 9-inch springform pan. Bake 5 minutes; cool completely.

For filling, beat cream cheese in a large bowl until fluffy. Gradually beat in 3/4 cup sugar. Add eggs, 1 at a time, beating well after each addition. Stir in lemon juice, lemon zest, and 2 teaspoons vanilla. Pour over crust. Bake 35 minutes. Combine sour cream, remaining 3 tablespoons sugar, and remaining 1 teaspoon vanilla in a small bowl; stir until well blended. Spread over cheesecake. Bake 15 minutes longer. Cool cheesecake 30 minutes on a wire rack.

For lemon glaze, combine sugar, cornstarch, and salt in a small saucepan. In a small bowl, combine water, lemon juice, and egg yolk; stir into sugar mixture. Stirring constantly, cook over medium-low heat until mixture comes to a boil and thickens. Remove from heat. Stir in butter, lemon zest, and food coloring; cool slightly. Spread over cheesecake. Cover and chill 8 hours. Remove sides of pan and garnish cheesecake with lemon curls.
Yield: 10 to 12 servings

SNOWMAN PIE BOX

You will need a pie box (we used a 10" square box), snowman-motif wrapping paper, dimensional paint to coordinate with wrapping paper, glue, and ribbons.

1. Following outlines of motifs, cut pieces and individual motifs from wrapping paper to fit on top and sides of box.
2. Glue wrapping paper pieces and motifs to box.
3. Use dimensional paint to outline some snowman motifs.
4. Place gift in box. Tie ribbons together into a bow around box; trim ends.

A "Soup-er" Gift

*D*eliver an abundance
of Christmas wishes with this
"soup-er" gift. The colorful
Dried Bean Soup Mix is made
with six types of beans to
symbolize the blessings of
health and prosperity. Layered
inside a glass jar, the beans will
make an appealing countertop
accent — and a hearty soup
when they're prepared with the
spicy seasoning mix and soup
recipe that you provide.

DRIED BEAN SOUP MIX AND SEASONING

DRIED BEAN MIX

$^1/_2$ cup of *each* of the following:
kidney beans, split yellow peas,
black beans, red lentils, small
red beans, and split green peas

SEASONING MIX

1 tablespoon dried sweet pepper
flakes

2 teaspoons chicken bouillon
granules

2 teaspoons dried minced onion

$1^1/_2$ teaspoons salt

1 teaspoon dried parsley flakes

$^1/_2$ teaspoon ground black pepper

$^1/_2$ teaspoon garlic powder

$^1/_2$ teaspoon celery seed

For dried bean mix, layer each type of
bean in a clear gift container.

For seasoning mix, combine all
ingredients. Store in a resealable plastic
bag. Give with recipe for Seasoned Bean
Soup.

Yield: about 3 cups dried bean mix and
about $^1/_4$ cup seasoning mix

SEASONED BEAN SOUP

Dried Bean Mix (3 cups)

2 cans ($14^1/_2$ ounces each) stewed
tomatoes

Seasoning Mix ($^1/_4$ cup)

Rinse beans and place in a large Dutch
oven. Pour 4 cups boiling water over
beans; cover and let soak overnight.

Drain beans and return to Dutch oven.
Add 6 cups water, cover, and bring to a
boil over high heat. Reduce heat to low
and simmer 1 to $1^1/_2$ hours or until beans
are almost tender. Add tomatoes and
seasoning mix. Stirring occasionally, cover
and simmer 30 minutes. Uncover beans
and continue to simmer about 1 hour
longer or until beans are tender and soup
thickens. Serve warm.

Yield: about 10 cups soup

PEACHY CHEESE BALL

*T*his clever appetizer is a "peachy" gift to share with friends. Formed into the shape of the mellow fruit, our Peachy Cheese Ball is a luscious blend of creamy cheeses, dried peaches, and peach brandy. Deliver the lightly sweet spread packed in a homey embellished crate along with crackers or butter cookies for serving.

PEACHY CHEESE BALL

- $^2/_3$ cup finely chopped dried peaches
- $^1/_3$ cup peach brandy
- 7 ounces Gouda cheese, finely shredded
- 4 ounces cream cheese, softened
- $^1/_3$ cup slivered almonds, toasted and finely ground
- 1 tablespoon peach preserves
- $^1/_4$ teaspoon ground cardamom
  Paprika, 2 toasted slivered almonds, and 2 green silk leaves to decorate
  Crackers or butter cookies

In a small saucepan, combine dried peaches and brandy. Cook over medium heat about 4 minutes or until mixture simmers. Stirring frequently, simmer uncovered 3 minutes longer or until liquid is absorbed. Remove from heat and cool.

In a medium bowl, combine Gouda cheese, cream cheese, ground almonds, peach preserves, cardamom, and peach mixture; beat until well blended. Divide mixture in half; cover and chill 30 minutes.

Shape each half to resemble a peach. Use a table knife to score from top to about halfway down each "peach." Use a pastry brush to pat a small amount of paprika onto cheese to give each cheese ball a peach color. Decorate each cheese ball with a slivered almond for a stem and a silk leaf. Cover and store in refrigerator. Serve with crackers or butter cookies.

Yield: 2 cheese balls, about 1 cup each

"PEACHY" CRATE

You will need a 6$^1/_2$" x 9$^1/_2$" wooden crate, light blue-green and blue-green spray paint, wood-tone spray, label cut from package of dried peaches, cream-colored paper, 1 yd of $^5/_8$"w ribbon, silk greenery, 6" of floral wire, glue, hole punch, black pen, and wood excelsior to line crate.

1. Spray paint crate blue-green.
2. Lightly spray paint crate light blue-green. Before paint dries, lightly spray crate with wood tone spray.
3. Glue label to paper. Cutting close to label, cut label from paper. Glue label to crate.
4. Use ribbon and follow *Making a Multi-Loop Bow*, page 123. Glue greenery and bow to crate. Line crate with excelsior.
5. For tag, cut tag shape from paper. Punch hole in tag. Use pen to write message on tag. Use a piece of excelsior to tie tag to bow.

CHEESY YULE LOG

*C*harm your favorite holiday hostess with this appetizing gift! Rolled in crispy toasted pecans, our Port Wine Cheese Log combines wine-soaked pieces of dried apple and two kinds of cheese. The piquant spread is presented in a rustic woodburned Noel basket. For a thoughtful finish, include an assortment of gourmet crackers with your surprise.

PORT WINE CHEESE LOG

$1/2$ cup finely chopped dried apples
5 tablespoons port wine
2 cups (8 ounces) shredded sharp Cheddar cheese
1 package (3 ounces) cream cheese, softened
$1/8$ teaspoon ground white pepper
$3/4$ cup coarsely chopped pecans, toasted
Crackers to serve

In a small bowl, combine apples and port wine. Cover and let stand 30 minutes or until wine is absorbed.

In a medium bowl, combine Cheddar cheese, cream cheese, and white pepper; beat about 3 minutes or until well blended. Stir in apple mixture. Cover and chill 1 hour.

Shape mixture into a 7-inch-long roll. Press pecans onto cheese. Wrap in plastic wrap. Store in refrigerator. Serve with crackers.

Yield: 1 cheese log, about $1^3/4$ cups

WOODBURNED "NOEL" BASKET

You will need an approx. 4" x 10$3/4$" x 2$1/4$" wooden basket with handle, a torn fabric piece to line basket, woodburning pen with universal and flow points (we used a Walnut Hollow Farm Creative Woodburner), silk holly pick, tracing paper, graphite transfer paper, soft eraser, and glue.

1. Trace "Noel" pattern, page 115, onto tracing paper. Use transfer paper to lightly transfer design to center of 1 side (front) of basket. If necessary, use eraser to erase smudge marks.
2. For border, use a pencil to draw alternating long ($1/4$") and short ($1/8$") lines along front edges of basket and angled lines at corners.
3. (*Caution:* Follow manufacturer's instructions when using woodburning pen. Allow the pen and point to cool completely before changing points. Practice woodburning on a wood scrap before working on project.) Use woodburning pen with flow point to burn small dots about $1/8$" apart along lines of letters and outlines of leaves. Burn wood 1 or 2 seconds longer to create larger dots for berries. Burn lines for veins on leaves. Change to universal point. Use sharp edge of point to burn border lines on basket.
4. Glue holly to 1 end of basket.
5. For liner, fringe edges of fabric piece about $1/2$" and place in basket.

DIVINE NO-BAKE COOKIES

*E*ach of these adorable packages delivers two wonderful Christmas surprises at once! The sweet angel bags are fashioned with glass doll head ornaments for holiday keepsakes. Tucked inside the winsome bags, our No-Bake Peanut Butter Cookies are deliciously easy to make and feature a yummy triple nutty taste. Gold chenille stems and starry ribbon add heavenly touches to your gift.

NO-BAKE PEANUT BUTTER COOKIES

- 1¹/₂ cups quick-cooking oats
- ¹/₂ cup flaked coconut
- ¹/₃ cup chopped peanuts
- ¹/₃ cup sugar
- ¹/₄ cup smooth peanut butter
- ¹/₄ cup vegetable oil
- 1 package (10 ounces) peanut butter chips

In a large bowl, combine oats, coconut, and peanuts. In a large saucepan, combine sugar, peanut butter, and oil over medium heat. Stirring constantly, cook until sugar dissolves. Remove from heat. Add peanut butter chips; stir until melted. Combine peanut butter mixture with oat mixture; stir just until moistened. Drop by rounded teaspoonfuls onto waxed paper. Chill about 30 minutes or until set. Store in an airtight container in a cool place.

Yield: about 3¹/₂ dozen cookies

ANGEL BAGS

For each bag, you will need a white lunch bag, a 2³/₄"h glass doll's head ornament, ⁷/₈ yd of 1¹/₂"w wired ribbon, 3 metallic gold chenille stems, rubber band, removable transparent tape, and glue.

1. Place gift in bag.
2. For collar, fold top of bag down about 1". Gather bag about 1" from fold and secure with rubber band. Fan top of bag out.
3. Tie ribbon length into a bow around bag, covering rubber band; trim ends.
4. For wings, form 2 chenille stems into heart shapes with ends at bottoms of hearts. Overlap ends of stems at back of bag and glue to secure.
5. For halo, cut a 6" length from remaining stem and form into a circle with a 1¹/₂" stem. Insert stem in top of ornament.
6. Use tape to secure doll's head ornament to top of bag.

NUTTY CARAMEL APPLE DESSERT

*H*ere's a tasty treat that will appeal to any cook on your Christmas list. Rich and gooey, Nutty Caramel Apple Dessert is created with a brown sugar-and-oat crust covered with a spicy apple mixture, walnuts, and caramel topping. It's especially good served with ice cream! Sponge-painted with apples, a plain canvas apron is a great gift that can be enjoyed all year.

NUTTY CARAMEL APPLE DESSERT

1¹/₂ cups all-purpose flour
1 teaspoon baking powder
¹/₂ teaspoon apple pie spice
¹/₄ teaspoon salt
1¹/₂ cups quick-cooking oats
1 cup firmly packed brown sugar
³/₄ cup chilled butter or margarine
1 can (20 ounces) sliced pie apples, drained and coarsely chopped
1 cup chopped walnuts
1 jar (12 ounces) caramel ice cream topping

Preheat oven to 375 degrees. In a medium bowl, combine flour, baking powder, apple pie spice, and salt. Stir in oats and brown sugar. Using a pastry blender or 2 knives, cut in butter until mixture is well blended. Reserve 1 cup oat mixture. Press remaining oat mixture into bottom of a lightly greased 9-inch square baking pan. Layer apples, reserved mixture, and walnuts. Drizzle with ice cream topping. Bake 30 to 35 minutes or until lightly browned and a toothpick

inserted into cake portion comes out clean. Cool in pan on a wire rack. Cover and store in a cool place. Give with serving instructions.

Yield: about 12 servings

To serve: Uncover and bake in a 325-degree oven 25 minutes or until heated through. Serve warm with vanilla ice cream.

APPLE APRON

You will need a canvas apron; yellow, red, green, and brown acrylic paint; compressed craft sponge; and tracing paper.

1. Trace apple, stem, leaf, and highlight patterns, page 115, separately onto tracing paper; cut out. Use patterns to cut shapes from sponge.
2. Lightly dampen sponge shapes. Use sponge shapes and follow *Sponge Painting*, page 121, to sponge paint red apples, brown stems, and green leaves on apron. Sponge paint yellow highlights on some apples.
3. Use a small sponge piece and green paint to sponge paint apron binding and ties.
4. Follow paint manufacturer's instructions to heat-set paint.

SPICY FRUIT CONSERVE

*D*eliver gifts of Dried
*Fruit Conserve to your neighbors
as sweet tokens of holiday
hospitality. The scrumptious
spread makes a tasty topping
for biscuits, muffins, or toast.
For gift-giving, embellish a plain
jar with a torn-fabric bow and a
hand-colored photocopied label.*

DRIED FRUIT CONSERVE

1½ cups chopped dried apricots
    (about 8 ounces)
1⅓ cups chopped dried peaches
    (about 8 ounces)
1⅓ cups chopped dried pears
    (about 8 ounces)
  1 medium unpeeled orange,
    seeded and chopped
  3 cups water
  2 cups sugar
 ½ cup raisins
  1 tablespoon freshly squeezed lemon
    juice
 ½ teaspoon ground cinnamon
 ⅛ teaspoon ground cloves
 ½ cup chopped pecans or walnuts

    In a large Dutch oven, combine
apricots, peaches, pears, orange, and
water over medium heat. Cover and cook
15 to 20 minutes or until fruit is tender.
Stir in sugar, raisins, lemon juice,
cinnamon, and cloves. Increase heat to
medium-high; bring mixture to a boil.
Stirring frequently, boil rapidly
10 minutes. Stir in pecans; cook
5 minutes longer or until mixture
thickens. Spoon into heat-resistant jars;
cover and cool to room temperature.
Store in refrigerator.

Yield: about 7 cups conserve

DECORATIVE JAR LID

You will need a 1" x 24" torn fabric
strip, a photocopy of jar lid insert design
(page 115) on cream paper, and colored
pencils.

1. Color photocopy of jar lid insert design
with colored pencils. Cut out insert.
2. Carefully unscrew band from filled jar.
Place insert over jar lid and replace band.
3. Tie fabric strip into a bow around jar
lid; trim ends.

CHEERY RAISIN-NUT DRESSING

A basket of fresh fruit and a jar of Raisin-Nut Dressing make a wonderful low-fat gift for a friend who's counting Christmas calories. The sweet, tangy dressing is also delicious served over salad greens. Just add matching bows to the jar and basket for a cheery offering.

RAISIN-NUT DRESSING

- ¹/₂ cup plus ¹/₄ cup unsweetened apple juice, divided
- 1 tablespoon cornstarch
- 3 tablespoons apple cider vinegar
- 3 tablespoons honey
- 1 tablespoon Dijon-style mustard
- 1 vanilla bean, split lengthwise
- ²/₃ cup golden raisins
- 2 tablespoons slivered almonds, toasted and chopped

In a small saucepan, combine ¹/₄ cup apple juice and cornstarch; stir until cornstarch dissolves. Gradually add remaining ¹/₂ cup apple juice; cook over medium heat until thickened and bubbly. Remove from heat. Whisk in vinegar, honey, and mustard. Scrape seeds from vanilla bean into apple juice mixture. Stir in raisins and almonds. Store in an airtight container in refrigerator. Serve chilled with fresh fruit salad or salad greens.

Yield: about 1¹/₂ cups dressing

*P*resented in one of these charming stamped tins, a gift of Chocolate-Raspberry-Almond Crunch is actually two treats in one! The delectable toffee offers a pleasing blend of favorite flavors, and the decorated containers are pretty Christmas keepsakes.

CHOCOLATE-RASPBERRY-ALMOND CRUNCH

    1   cup butter
    1   cup sugar
    1/3 cup water
    1   tablespoon light corn syrup
    3   cups sliced almonds, toasted and
        divided
    1/2 teaspoon vanilla extract
    1/2 teaspoon almond extract
    1   cup raspberry-flavored semisweet
        chocolate chips, divided

Line 2 baking sheets with aluminum foil; grease foil. Butter sides of a very heavy large saucepan. Combine butter, sugar, water, and corn syrup in saucepan. Stirring constantly, cook over medium-low heat until sugar dissolves. Using a pastry brush dipped in hot water, wash down any sugar crystals on sides of pan. Attach a candy thermometer to pan, making sure thermometer does not touch bottom of pan. Increase heat to medium and bring to a boil. Cook, without stirring, until mixture reaches hard-crack stage (approximately 300 to 310 degrees). Test about 1/2 teaspoon mixture in ice water. Mixture will form brittle threads in ice water and will remain brittle when removed from the water. Remove from heat and stir in 1 cup almonds and extracts. Spread mixture on 1 baking sheet. Sprinkle 1/2 cup chocolate chips over hot candy; spread melted chocolate with a knife. Sprinkle 1 cup almonds over chocolate; press into chocolate. Invert toffee onto second baking sheet. Remove foil and sprinkle second side with remaining 1/2 cup chocolate chips; spread melted chocolate with a knife. Sprinkle remaining 1 cup almonds over chocolate; press into chocolate. Chill candy 1 hour or until chocolate hardens.

Break into small pieces. Store in an airtight container between layers of waxed paper in a cool place.

Yield: about 1 3/4 pounds candy

STAMPED POINSETTIA TINS

You will need light-colored fabric; 1 1/4 yds of 1 3/8"w plaid wired ribbon; gold trim; green spray paint; an approx. 4"h poinsettia rubber stamp; black fabric paint; foam brush; yellow, red, light green, and green fabric markers; black permanent felt-tip pen (if needed); and glue.

For canister, you will *also* need a tin canister at least 5" high and poster board.
For tin, you will *also* need a round tin at least 5" in diameter, polyester bonded batting, and a fabric marking pen.

CANISTER

1. Spray paint outside of lid green.
2. With lid on canister, measure height to bottom of lid. Measure around canister and add 1". Cut a piece of poster board the determined size. Cut a piece of fabric 1" larger on all sides than poster board.
3. Center poster board piece on wrong side of fabric. Fold edges of fabric over edges of poster board; glue in place.
4. (*Note:* Practice stamping technique on scrap fabric before stamping project.) To stamp design on fabric, slightly dilute black paint with water. Use foam brush to lightly apply diluted paint to raised surface of stamp. Firmly press stamp at center of fabric-covered poster board; allow to dry.
5. (*Note:* When using fabric markers, use light pressure to keep color from bleeding outside stamped lines. To darken an area of design, apply marker to area again. If necessary, use black pen to darken outlines of poinsettia.) Use markers to color poinsettia.
6. Wrap fabric-covered poster board around canister and glue in place.
7. Glue trim along top of fabric-covered poster board.
8. Tie ribbon into a bow; trim ends. Glue bow to lid.

TIN

1. Spray paint outside of tin green.
2. For lid, use fabric marking pen to draw around lid on batting and wrong side of fabric. Cut out batting circle along drawn circle and fabric circle about 1/2" outside drawn circle.
3. Place fabric circle right side up on a protected surface. Follow Steps 4 and 5 of Canister instructions to stamp and color design on fabric circle.
4. Glue batting to top of lid. Center fabric circle on lid and glue edges to sides of lid. If necessary, trim edges of fabric just above bottom of lid.
5. Glue trim to side of lid, covering edges of fabric. Glue trim along bottom edge of tin.
6. Tie ribbon into a bow; trim ends. Glue bow to lid.

SASSY BARBECUED PEANUTS

*A*dd sass to Christmas snacking by giving bags of fiery Barbecued Peanuts! The tasty nuts are baked in a spicy coating and sprinkled with brown sugar for a lightly sweet finish. For sharing, place the nuts in plain paper sacks embellished with fused-on appliqués, pen "stitching," buttons, and raffia.

BARBECUED PEANUTS

$1/4$ cup Worcestershire sauce
3 tablespoons vegetable oil
$1/2$ cup plus 6 tablespoons firmly packed brown sugar, divided
$1^1/2$ teaspoons dried minced onion
1 teaspoon apple cider vinegar
1 teaspoon hot pepper sauce
1 teaspoon garlic powder
$1/4$ teaspoon ground red pepper
2 containers (12 ounces each) lightly salted peanuts

Preheat oven to 250 degrees. In a heavy large skillet, combine Worcestershire sauce and oil. Stir in $1/2$ cup brown sugar, onion, vinegar, pepper sauce, garlic powder, and red pepper. Stirring frequently, cook over medium heat about 3 minutes or until sugar dissolves. Remove from heat. Add peanuts; stir until well coated. Spread peanut mixture in a $10^1/2$ x $15^1/2$-inch jellyroll pan. Bake 1 hour, stirring every 10 minutes. Sprinkle remaining 6 tablespoons brown sugar over hot peanuts; toss until coated. Spread on lightly greased aluminum foil to cool. Store in an airtight container.

Yield: about 7 cups peanuts

COUNTRY GIFT SACKS

For each sack, you will need a small brown paper bag, fabric(s) for appliqué(s), fusible web, assorted buttons, black felt-tip pen, natural raffia, hole punch, glue, and a $1^1/4$"w wooden star button (for tree appliqué sack only).

1. Use either star and heart or tree patterns, page 117, and follow *Making Appliqués*, page 121, to make appliqué(s) from fabric(s).
2. Fuse appliqué(s) to front of bag. Use pen to draw stitches around appliqué. Glue button(s) to appliqué(s).
3. Place gift in bag. Fold top of bag about $1^1/4$" to front. Punch 2 holes close together at center of folded part of bag.
4. For star sack, thread several lengths of raffia through holes in bag and tie into a bow at front. Thread a length of raffia through holes in a button and knot at back; trim ends close to knot. Glue button to bow.
5. For tree sack, fuse web to wrong side of a small fabric piece. Use star button as a pattern to cut shape from fabric. Fuse shape to button. Thread several lengths of raffia through holes in bag and button and knot at front of button; trim ends.

CINNAMON MOCHA MIX

*B*rew up a flurry of fun with bags of Cinnamon Mocha Mix. The yummy beverage starter combines chocolate mix for milk, instant coffee, and cinnamon with non-dairy creamer. And since our recipe makes plenty, you'll have lots of quick gifts. The cute bags are decorated with ribbon and hand-colored tags.

CINNAMON MOCHA MIX

1   jar (16 ounces) non-dairy
     powdered creamer
1   package (16 ounces) chocolate
     mix for milk
1   package (16 ounces)
     confectioners sugar
6   cups nonfat dry milk powder
$1/2$ cup cocoa
$1/4$ cup instant coffee granules
2   teaspoons ground cinnamon

In a very large bowl, combine creamer, chocolate mix, confectioners sugar, dry milk, cocoa, coffee granules, and cinnamon. Store in an airtight container. Give with serving instructions.

Yield: about 14 cups mix

To serve: Pour 6 ounces hot water over $2^1/2$ heaping tablespoons mocha mix; stir until well blended. Serve hot.

SNOWY GIFT BAGS

For each bag, you will need a small white gift bag (our bags measure 3" x 6½"), ⅞"w metallic silver ribbon, 10" of ¼"w blue ribbon, photocopy of tag design (page 123), blue paper, blue colored pencil, black felt-tip pen, stapler, and glue.

1. Glue a length of silver ribbon around bag from center top of front to center top of back.

2. Place gift in bag. Fold top of bag about ½" to back and staple closed. Tie blue ribbon into a bow; trim ends. Glue bow over staple.

3. For tag, use blue pencil to color photocopy of tag design. Use pen to write "Cinnamon Mocha Mix" on tag. Cut out tag. Glue tag to blue paper. Cutting close to tag, cut tag from paper. Glue tag to bag.

"Happy Hour" Basket

*B*ring an impromptu holiday "happy hour" to favorite neighbors when you present them with this basket of flavorful appetizers. Our easy Pickled Carrots and Pickled Asparagus are zesty tidbits for serving with the cheese, crackers, and wine that accompany them. Each recipe makes several gifts, so you can spread cheer all around your block!

PICKLED CARROTS

1½ cups apple cider vinegar
1½ cups water
 1 cup sugar
 2 pounds peeled baby carrots
    (about 6 cups)
 2 tablespoons dill seed
 3 to 4 cloves garlic

In a non-aluminum Dutch oven combine vinegar, water, and sugar. Stirring constantly, bring mixture to a boil over medium heat. Add carrots, dill seed, and garlic; return mixture to a boil. Reduce heat to low. Cover and simmer 8 minutes. Spoon into 6 heat-resistant jars; cover and cool to room temperature. Chill 8 hours to allow flavors to blend. Store in refrigerator.

Yield: about 6 cups carrots

PICKLED ASPARAGUS

 3 pounds fresh asparagus
    Fresh dill weed sprigs
    Strips of lemon zest
 4 cups water
 1 cup white vinegar
¼ cup canning and pickling salt

Cut asparagus into 3½-inch spears. Pack asparagus, dill weed, and lemon strips into each of 8 heat-resistant half-pint jars. In a non-aluminum large saucepan, combine water, vinegar, and canning salt. Bring mixture to a boil over medium-high heat. Pour liquid over vegetables; cover and cool to room temperature. Store in refrigerator.

Yield: about 8 cups asparagus

For jar lids, follow *Jar Lid Finishing,* page 122.

PEACH-ALMOND SCONES

*T*his year, deliver holiday greetings with a hint of international flair! Our Peach-Almond Scones are a fruity variation of a traditional Scottish quick bread. Cut into triangles before baking, the lightly sweet scones are ideal for breakfast on the go or afternoon tea. As a Christmas bonus, include a fingertip towel featuring cross-stitched angels. The charming piece makes a heavenly accent for the kitchen or bath.

PEACH-ALMOND SCONES

- 1 package (7 ounces) dried peaches, finely chopped
- 1/3 cup orange juice
- 2 1/4 cups all-purpose flour
- 1/3 cup firmly packed brown sugar
- 2 1/4 teaspoons baking powder
- 1/2 teaspoon salt
- 1/2 cup chilled butter
- 1/4 cup whipping cream
- 1 egg
- 1 teaspoon vanilla extract
- 1/2 cup sliced almonds

Preheat oven to 375 degrees. In a small microwave-safe bowl, combine peaches and orange juice. Cover and microwave on high power (100%) 2 minutes or until juice is hot; set aside. In a large bowl, combine flour, brown sugar, baking powder, and salt; stir until well blended. Using a pastry blender or 2 knives, cut in butter until mixture resembles coarse meal. In a small bowl, combine whipping cream, egg, and vanilla. Make a well in center of dry ingredients. Add whipping

cream mixture, peaches, and almonds; stir just until moistened. On a greased baking sheet, shape dough into a 9-inch-diameter circle. Use a serrated knife to cut dough into 8 wedges (do not separate wedges). Bake 22 to 27 minutes or until lightly browned and a toothpick inserted in center of bread comes out clean. Serve warm or transfer to a wire rack to cool completely.

Yield: 8 scones

ANGEL TOWEL

You will need an ecru fingertip towel with Aida (14 ct) insert and embroidery floss (see color key, page 116).

Center and stitch angel design, page 116, on towel insert, using 3 strands of floss for Cross Stitch and 1 strand for Backstitch and French Knots.

SPICY FIRESIDE BULLSHOT

*L*et the winter winds blow — a lucky friend will stay nice and toasty while sipping Spicy Fireside Bullshot! Served warm, this unusually delicious drink can be enjoyed with or without vodka for a palate-pleasing taste. A fast-to-finish cross-stitched mug lends Christmas spirit to the delightful beverage basket.

SPICY FIRESIDE BULLSHOT

    1   can (46 ounces) vegetable juice
    2   cans (14.5 ounces each) beef broth
    1   tablespoon steak sauce
    2   teaspoons lemon pepper
  $^1/_2$ teaspoon celery salt

In a 3-quart container, combine vegetable juice, beef broth, steak sauce, lemon pepper, and celery salt. Cover and store in refrigerator overnight to let flavors blend. Give with serving instructions.

Yield: about 8$^1/_2$ cups drink mixture

To serve: In a large saucepan, heat drink mixture until hot. Serve plain or add 1$^1/_2$ ounces vodka to each 8-ounce serving of hot drink mixture.

CHRISTMAS MUG

You will need a red Mugs Your Way™ mug, a white Vinyl-Weave™ mug insert (14 count), and embroidery floss (see color key, page 116).

Center and stitch mug design, page 116, on insert, using 3 strands of floss for Cross Stitch. Place insert in mug with ends at back.

MERRY CHERRY WINE

*S*teeped with Christmas
spirit, our Merry Cherry Wine
is a cordial way to say "Happy
Holidays!" Maraschino cherries
are infused in white wine and
cherry brandy for the sweet,
zippy liqueur. A matching
bottle label and gift tag, gilded
using rubber stamps, add a
stylish touch. Embellish the
basket with faux berries and
gold cord and include a
jar of the marinated cherries
for serving with the wine.

MERRY CHERRY WINE

  1 bottle (750 ml) dry white wine
  1 jar (10 ounces) red maraschino
      cherries
$^1/_4$ cup cherry brandy

In a 2-quart container, combine wine,
undrained cherries, and brandy. Cover
and allow mixture to stand at room
temperature 24 hours.

Return cherries to cherry jar. Pour
cherry wine into gift bottle. Store cherries
and wine in refrigerator. Serve wine with a
cherry in each glass.

Yield: about 4 cups wine

PEACH AND APRICOT SAUCE

*S*atisfy the dessert lover on your Christmas list with a gift of yummy Peach and Apricot Sauce. Flavored with cinnamon and nutmeg, this spirited topping is quick and easy to make using canned fruit. Because the sauce is especially flavorful over cake, why not include an angel food loaf with your gift so your friend can enjoy the goodness right away!

PEACH AND APRICOT SAUCE

- 1 can (16 ounces) sliced peaches in syrup, drained
- 1 can (16 ounces) apricots in syrup, drained
- $1/2$ cup water
- $1/4$ cup sugar
- 2 tablespoons cornstarch
- 1 tablespoon freshly squeezed lemon juice
- 2 tablespoons bourbon
- $1/4$ teaspoon ground cinnamon
- $1/8$ teaspoon ground nutmeg

Process peaches and apricots in a food processor until smooth. In a medium saucepan, combine water, sugar, cornstarch, and lemon juice; stir until smooth. Stir in puréed fruit. Stirring constantly, cook over medium heat about 5 minutes or until thick and bubbly. Remove from heat; whisk in bourbon, cinnamon, and nutmeg. Serve warm or chilled over angel food cake or frozen yogurt.

Yield: about 2$1/2$ cups sauce

For tag, follow *Making a Tag,* page 123.

BUTTERED PEPPER PASTA

A great gift for a friend on the go, our Christmas Pepper Pasta will be a quick-to-fix meal during the holiday rush. The homemade pasta, flavored with sweet red and green peppers, cooks in just a few minutes, and our Cilantro Butter adds just the right touch of seasoning. Adorn the decorative jar with a wooden pasta spoon and sprigs of greenery for a tasteful presentation.

CHRISTMAS PEPPER PASTA

Make pasta recipe twice using sweet red pepper and green pepper.

    Olive oil
  1 large sweet red pepper *or* green pepper, coarsely chopped
  1 egg
  2 teaspoons olive oil
  $1/2$ teaspoon salt
$1^3/_4$ cups all-purpose flour

Preheat oven to 400 degrees. Lightly grease an 8-inch square baking pan with olive oil. Place pepper in pan; cover and bake 45 minutes or until pepper is soft, stirring every 15 minutes. Cool in pan.

Process cooked pepper in a large food processor until puréed. Measure and return $1/3$ cup purée to processor. Save remaining purée for another use. Add egg, 2 teaspoons oil, and salt; process until well blended. Add flour; process until dough sticks together and forms a ball. Process 1 minute longer. Remove from processor and shape into a smooth ball; cover with plastic wrap and let rest 30 minutes.

If using a pasta machine, follow manufacturer's instructions to make pasta.

If rolling dough by hand, divide dough into fourths. Cover dough with a damp towel or plastic wrap to prevent drying. Working with one fourth of dough at a time, use a rolling pin to roll dough into a 6 x 14-inch rectangle. Allow dough to dry about 5 minutes.

Beginning at 1 short edge, fold dough into thirds (dough will be about a 6 x $4^1/_2$-inch rectangle). Beginning at one $4^1/_2$-inch side, cut dough into $1/4$-inch-wide pieces; separate strands. Dry pasta on a towel-covered flat surface about 6 hours. Store in an airtight container in a cool place up to 2 weeks. Give with serving instructions.

Yield: about 18 ounces dried pasta

To serve: In a large Dutch oven, bring 4 quarts water to a boil; stir in 1 tablespoon salt. Add dried pasta to boiling water. Return water to a boil and cook 7 to 15 minutes or until pasta is tender but firm; drain. Add Cilantro Butter to warm pasta; toss until butter melts. Serve immediately.

Yield: about 9 cups cooked pasta

CILANTRO BUTTER

  $1/2$ cup butter, softened
  $1/2$ cup chopped fresh cilantro
  1 tablespoon freshly squeezed lemon juice
  $1/2$ teaspoon ground cumin
  $1/4$ teaspoon ground white pepper
  1 clove garlic, minced

In a small bowl, combine butter, cilantro, lemon juice, cumin, white pepper, and garlic. Cover and store in refrigerator.

Yield: about $3/4$ cup cilantro butter

To serve: Toss butter with warm Christmas Pepper Pasta; serve immediately.

HEAVEN-SENT BRITTLE

*H*ere's a sweet gift for a friend who's heaven-sent! Crunchy, buttery Cinnamon Almond Brittle is loaded with crispy nuts. Embellished with tiny cherubs, the gift boxes are spray painted, spattered with gold paint, and then finished with gilded ivy leaves and golden bows.

CINNAMON ALMOND BRITTLE

- 2 cups sugar
- ³/₄ cup light corn syrup
- ¹/₄ cup water
- 3 cups whole almonds, toasted and coarsely chopped
- 3 tablespoons butter
- 2 teapoons ground cinnamon
- 1 teaspoon vanilla extract
- ¹/₂ teaspoon salt
- 1¹/₂ teaspoons baking soda

Butter sides of a heavy large saucepan. Combine sugar, corn syrup, and water in saucepan. Stirring constantly, cook over medium-low heat until sugar dissolves. Using a pastry brush dipped in hot water, wash down any sugar crystals on sides of pan. Attach a candy thermometer to pan, making sure thermometer does not touch bottom of pan. Increase heat to medium and bring to a boil. Cook, without stirring, until mixture reaches hard-crack stage (approximately 300 to 310 degrees) and turns light golden in color. Test about ¹/₂ teaspoon mixture in ice water. Mixture will form brittle threads in ice water and will remain brittle when removed from

the water. Stir in almonds. Remove from heat and stir in butter, cinnamon, vanilla, and salt; stir until butter melts. Stir in baking soda (mixture may foam). Pour mixture onto a large piece of greased aluminum foil placed on a dampened flat surface. Use 2 wooden spoons to pull warm candy until stretched thin. Cool completely. Break into pieces. Store in an airtight container.

Yield: about 2¹/₄ pounds candy

ANGELIC BOXES

For each box, you will need an approx. 4³/₄"w heart-shaped papier-mâché box with lid, a 3³/₈"w plaster cherub, red spray paint, metallic gold acrylic paint, paintbrush, an old toothbrush, 10" of gold cord, wired silk holly garland, wire cutters, paper towels, and glue.

1. Spray paint box red.
2. (*Note:* Practice spatter painting on scrap paper before painting project.) To spatter paint lid gold, dilute gold paint slightly with water. Dip toothbrush in paint and pull thumb across bristles.
3. Use paintbrush to paint cherub gold.
4. Glue cherub to lid. Glue holly along edges of lid. Tie cord into a bow and knot and trim streamers; glue to lid.
5. For additional gold accents, dip paintbrush in gold paint, then brush on paper towel to remove most of paint. Use "dry" brush to lightly paint box and holly.

CHRISTMAS BRUNCH JAM

A delightful blend of flavors, Christmas Brunch Jam offers a delicious way to spread Yuletide cheer. The tartness of cranberries, lemon juice, and fresh Granny Smith apple is complemented with sweet crushed pineapple. The tangy spread is great served with English muffins, biscuits, or toast.

CHRISTMAS BRUNCH JAM

- 3 cups fresh cranberries
- 1 can (20 ounces) crushed pineapple in heavy syrup
- 1 cup peeled and diced Granny Smith apple
- 3 cups sugar
- 1½ cups water
- 2 tablespoons freshly squeezed lemon juice
- 1¾ teaspoons grated lemon zest

Combine cranberries, undrained pineapple, apple, sugar, water, lemon juice, and lemon zest in a Dutch oven. Stirring constantly, cook over medium-low heat until sugar dissolves. Attach a candy thermometer to pan, making sure thermometer does not touch bottom of pan. Stirring frequently, cook uncovered until mixture reaches 221 degrees (about 1½ hours). Spoon into heat-resistant jars; cover and cool to room temperature. Store in refrigerator.

Yield: about 5 cups jam

SWEET AND SAVORY ROLLS

How does Mrs. Claus reward Santa's reindeer on Christmas morning? With gifts of her homemade Sweet and Savory Spiral Rolls, of course! And you can deliver those same treats on Christmas Eve as next-morning nibbles for special families on your holiday list. The basic yeast dough recipe makes three pans of rolls, which can each be prepared with one of our three sweet or savory fillings. Wrap the rolls in cellophane and tie on a festive reindeer ornament for an eye-opening offering.

SWEET AND SAVORY SPIRAL ROLLS

YEAST DOUGH

  1 package quick-acting dry yeast
$1/4$ cup plus 1 teaspoon sugar, divided
$1/4$ cup warm water
$13/4$ cups milk
$1/3$ cup butter or margarine
  1 teaspoon salt
  5 to 6 cups all-purpose flour, divided
  1 egg
    Vegetable cooking spray

PARMESAN-HERB FILLING

  3 tablespoons butter or margarine
  2 cloves garlic, minced
  2 teaspoons dried Italian seasoning
$1/4$ cup freshly grated Parmesan cheese

CINNAMON-PECAN FILLING

$1/3$ cup firmly packed brown sugar
  2 teaspoons ground cinnamon
  4 tablespoons butter or margarine,
    softened
$1/2$ cup chopped pecans

APRICOT-ALMOND FILLING

$1/2$ cup apricot preserves
$1/4$ cup sugar
$1/2$ cup sliced almonds

VANILLA GLAZE

$1/2$ cup sifted confectioners sugar
  2 teaspoons water
$1/2$ teaspoon vanilla extract

ALMOND GLAZE

$1/2$ cup sifted confectioners sugar
  2 teaspoons water
$1/2$ teaspoon almond extract

In a small bowl, dissolve yeast and 1 teaspoon sugar in $1/4$ cup warm water. In a small saucepan, heat milk, butter, remaining $1/4$ cup sugar, and salt over medium heat until butter melts; remove from heat. In a large bowl, combine 2 cups flour and milk mixture. Beat in yeast mixture and egg; beat until well blended. Add 3 cups flour, 1 cup at a time; stir until a soft dough forms. Turn onto a lightly floured surface. Knead about 5 minutes or until dough becomes smooth and elastic, using additional flour as necessary. Place in a large bowl sprayed with cooking spray, turning once to coat top of dough. Cover and let rise in a warm place (80 to 85 degrees) $11/4$ hours or until doubled in size.

Turn dough onto a lightly floured surface and punch down. Divide dough into thirds. Roll each third into a 10 x 14-inch rectangle. Spread each rectangle with 1 of the following fillings:

For Parmesan-herb filling, combine butter, garlic, and Italian seasoning in a small microwave-safe bowl. Microwave on medium power (50%) 1 minute; stir until butter melts. Cover and allow to stand 10 minutes for flavors to blend. Brush dough with herb butter mixture. Sprinkle Parmesan cheese over dough.

For cinnamon-pecan filling, combine brown sugar and cinnamon in a small bowl. Spread butter on dough. Sprinkle with brown sugar mixture. Sprinkle with pecans.

For apricot-almond filling, combine apricot preserves and sugar in a small bowl; stir until well blended. Spread apricot mixture on dough. Sprinkle with almonds.

Beginning at 1 short edge, roll up each rectangle jellyroll style. Pinch seams to seal. Cut dough into 1-inch slices. Place each type of roll, cut side down, in a greased 8-inch round cake pan. Spray rolls with cooking spray, cover, and let rise in a warm place about 40 minutes or until doubled in size.

Preheat oven to 350 degrees. Bake 20 to 27 minutes or until golden brown. Cool in pans 10 minutes. Remove rolls from pans. Serve Parmesan-herb rolls warm or cool completely.

For vanilla glaze, combine confectioners sugar, water, and vanilla in a small bowl; stir until smooth. Drizzle glaze over warm cinnamon-pecan rolls. Serve warm or cool completely.

For almond glaze, combine confectioners sugar, water, and almond extract in a small bowl; stir until smooth. Drizzle glaze over warm apricot-almond rolls. Serve warm or cool completely.

Yield: 3 pans, 10 rolls each

REINDEER ORNAMENT

You will need one 6" square each of red fabric, muslin, and low-loft cotton batting; fusible web; 6" of $1/4$"w ribbon for hanger; red, green, tan, and metallic gold acrylic paint; stencil brushes; small paintbrush; acetate for stencils; black permanent felt-tip pen with fine point; craft knife and cutting mat; tracing paper; graphite transfer paper; pressing cloth; and glue.

1. Fuse web to wrong sides of fabric squares. Fuse red fabric to batting. Do not remove paper backing from muslin.
2. To stencil reindeer on muslin, use pattern, page 117, and follow *Stenciling*, page 121, to stencil head, antlers, and bow tie.
3. Trace detail lines of pattern (shown in grey) onto tracing paper. Use transfer paper to transfer detail lines to reindeer. Use pen to outline stenciled shapes, draw over transferred detail lines, and color eyes. Paint nose and beads red.
4. Cutting close to design, cut reindeer from muslin square. Using pressing cloth, fuse reindeer to center of red fabric square. Cutting about $1/4$" from reindeer, cut reindeer from red fabric.
5. For hanger, fold ribbon in half and glue ends to top back of reindeer.

ELEGANT EGGNOG FUDGE

*A*ll the tasty goodness of a favorite Christmas beverage is stirred into our remarkably creamy Eggnog Fudge. For stunning presentations, place pieces of fudge in individual candy cups and pack them in clear candy boxes. Lengths of golden ribbons, cord, and charms decorate these magnificent holiday tokens.

EGGNOG FUDGE

  3 cups sugar
1¹/₂ cups whipping cream
 ¹/₄ cup light corn syrup
 ¹/₈ teaspoon salt
  2 tablespoons butter
  2 teaspoons vanilla extract
 ¹/₂ teaspoon brandy extract
 ³/₄ teaspoon freshly grated nutmeg

Line an 8-inch square baking pan with aluminum foil, extending foil over 2 sides of pan; grease foil. Butter sides of a heavy large saucepan. Combine sugar, whipping cream, corn syrup, and salt in saucepan. Stirring constantly, cook over medium-low heat until sugar dissolves. Using a pastry brush dipped in hot water, wash down any sugar crystals on sides of pan. Attach a candy thermometer to pan, making sure thermometer does not touch bottom of pan. Increase heat to medium and bring to a boil. Cook, without stirring, until mixture reaches soft-ball stage (approximately 234 to 240 degrees). Test about ¹/₂ teaspoon mixture in ice water. Mixture will easily form a ball in ice water but will flatten when held in your hand. Place pan in 2 inches of cold water in sink. Add butter, extracts, and nutmeg; do not stir. Cool to approximately 110 degrees. Remove from sink. Using medium speed of an electric mixer, beat about 6 minutes or until fudge thickens and begins to lose its gloss. Pour into prepared pan. Cover and chill about 4 hours or until firm.

Cut into 1-inch squares. Store in an airtight container in refrigerator.

Yield: about 4 dozen pieces fudge

HEAVENLY BARS

*I*f angels indulged in sweets, surely they would nibble on our Heavenly Bars! The chocolaty layered squares are delivered in a gilded tin that's embellished with stickers and gold paint. Netting, starry ribbon, and an easy-to-make tag complete the package.

HEAVENLY BARS

72 butter-flavored rectangular crackers (half of a 16-ounce package), divided
 1 cup butter or margarine
¹/₂ cup milk
 2 cups graham cracker crumbs
 1 cup firmly packed brown sugar
¹/₃ cup granulated sugar
²/₃ cup smooth peanut butter
¹/₂ cup milk chocolate chips
¹/₂ cup semisweet chocolate chips

Line a 9 x 13-inch baking pan with aluminum foil, extending foil over ends of pan; grease foil. Place a layer of 24 crackers in bottom of pan. Melt butter in a heavy medium saucepan over medium-high heat. Stir in milk, graham cracker crumbs, and sugars. Bring mixture to a boil. Reduce heat to medium. Stirring constantly, boil 5 minutes. Remove from heat. Spread half of sugar mixture over crackers. Place another layer of 24 crackers in pan. Spread remaining sugar mixture over crackers. Top with another layer of crackers. In a small saucepan, combine peanut butter and chocolate chips. Stirring frequently, cook over low heat until mixture is smooth. Spread chocolate mixture over crackers. Cover and chill about 4 hours or until firm.

Lift from pan using ends of foil. Cut into 1¹/₂-inch squares. Store in an airtight container in refrigerator.

Yield: about 4 dozen squares

ANGEL TIN

You will need a 6¹/₂" dia. tin with lid, a 6" x 27" strip of white netting, ¹/₂ yd of 1¹/₂"w wired ribbon, angel stickers, metallic gold spray paint, metallic gold and dark gold liquid acrylic paint, small natural sponge pieces, matte clear acrylic spray, and cream paper for tag.

1. Spray paint tin gold.
2. For tag, fold a piece of cream paper in half.
3. Apply stickers to tag and lid of tin.
4. Using sponge pieces and metallic gold and dark gold paint, follow *Sponge Painting*, page 121, to sponge-paint tin and tag.
5. Apply 2 coats of acrylic spray to tin.
6. Knot netting strip around tin. Tie ribbon into a bow around ends of netting; trim ends of ribbon.

SPICY BARBECUE SNACK MIX

Happy Yule Y'all!

*B*uckaroos of all ages will let out a hearty "Ya-hoo!" when they get a taste of our fiery Barbecue Snack Mix! The super-crunchy munchies are baked with a blend of twelve spices for a flavor that's sure to cause a taste bud stampede. To share this gift, round up some of the prepared snack mix in our bandanna-covered gift bag. Don't forget to tie on a sackful of the Barbecue Spice Mix and share the recipe for the snacks, so the cowpoke can rustle up a batch back home on the range.

BARBECUE SPICE MIX

1	cup paprika
3/4	cup firmly packed brown sugar
1	tablespoon ground black pepper
1	tablespoon garlic powder
2	teaspoons chili powder
2	teaspoons ground ginger
1	teaspoon ground nutmeg
1	teaspoon salt
1/2	teaspoon ground thyme
1/2	teaspoon onion powder
1/2	teaspoon celery seed
1/4	teaspoon ground coriander
1/4	teaspoon ground red pepper
1/4	teaspoon ground cloves

Combine all ingredients in a small bowl; stir until well blended. Store in an airtight container. Give with recipe for Barbecue Snack Mix.

Yield: about 2 cups spice mix

BARBECUE SNACK MIX

3	cups square corn cereal
3	cups small pretzel twists
3	cups corn chips
3	cups cheese snack crackers
2	cups lightly salted peanuts
1/2	cup butter or margarine
1	tablespoon Worcestershire sauce
1/4	cup Barbecue Spice Mix

Preheat oven to 250 degrees. Combine corn cereal, pretzels, corn chips, cheese crackers, and peanuts in a large roasting pan. In a small saucepan, melt butter over medium-low heat. Remove from heat and stir in Worcestershire sauce and spice mix. Pour butter mixture over cereal mixture; stir until well coated. Bake 1 hour, stirring every 15 minutes. Spread on aluminum foil to cool. Store in an airtight container.

Yield: about 14 cups snack mix

ROUNDUP BROWN BAG

You will need a brown gift bag with handles removed, a penny sack, a red bandanna, fusible web, 4"w red wooden star ornament, silk pine spray, jute twine, 6" of craft wire, red and black felt-tip pens, and a hole punch.

1. Fuse web to wrong side of bandanna. Cut a piece from bandanna to fit front of gift bag. Fuse bandanna piece to front of bag.
2. Place snack mix in bag. Punch 2 holes close together through top of bag. Thread a length of twine through holes in bag and knot at front. Use a second length of twine and follow Step 1 of *Making a Multi-Loop Bow*, page 123. Knot ends of twine on bag around bow to secure.
3. Use black pen to write "Happy Yule Y'all!" and red pen to draw stars on penny sack. Place spice mix in sack. Knot a length of twine around top of sack and tie sack to bow on bag.
4. Tuck pine spray behind bow on bag. Thread wire length through hanger on ornament and wire ornament to pine spray to secure.

FLAVORFUL MIXES

*F*riends who enjoy sampling a variety of tastes will savor these flavorful mixes. Used in place of curry powder, Caribbean Spice Mix brings a hint of the islands to recipes. Buttermilk Dressing, a true Southern specialty, is tasty served on salads or as a vegetable dip. Finish each bag of mix with a colorful label and a wooden spoon for a clever delivery.

CARIBBEAN SPICE MIX

- 1/4 cup ground turmeric
- 2 tablespoons ground coriander
- 1 tablespoon ground cumin
- 1 tablespoon ground cinnamon
- 2 1/4 teaspoons ground ginger
- 2 1/4 teaspoons garlic powder
- 1 teaspoon ground black pepper
- 1/2 teaspoon ground cloves

Combine all ingredients in a small bowl; stir until well blended. Store in an airtight container. Substitute for curry powder in recipes.

Yield: about 1/2 cup spice mix

BUTTERMILK DRESSING MIX

- 2 tablespoons dried thyme leaves
- 1 1/2 tablespoons dried parsley flakes
- 1 tablespoon lemon pepper
- 2 teaspoons salt
- 1 teaspoon dried sage leaves
- 1 teaspoon garlic powder
- 1 teaspoon ground black pepper

Process all ingredients in a small food processor until well blended. Store in an airtight container. Give with serving instructions.

Yield: about 1/4 cup dressing mix

To serve: For salad dressing, combine 1 1/2 teaspoons dressing mix, 1/2 cup buttermilk, and 1/2 cup mayonnaise; stir until blended. Cover and chill 1 hour to allow flavors to blend.

For dip, combine 1 1/2 teaspoons dressing mix, 1/2 cup sour cream, and 1/2 cup mayonnaise; stir until blended. Cover and chill 1 hour to allow flavors to blend.

SPOON-TOPPED GIFT SACKS

For each sack, you will need a small gift sack (ours measure 3" x 6 1/2"), 3/8 yd of 1/4"w grosgrain ribbon, wooden spoon, small glass ball ornament, white paper, black felt-tip pen, colored pencils, a stapler, and glue.

1. For label, use pen to trace desired design, page 118, onto white paper. Use colored pencils to color label. Cut out label.
2. Place gift in sack. Fold top of sack about 1 3/4" to back and staple twice about 1" from fold. Glue label to top front of sack. Slide handle of spoon between fold and staples.
3. Thread ornament onto ribbon. Tie ribbon into a bow around spoon handle; trim ends.

SANTA'S PET SNACKS

Santa doesn't forget his four-legged friends at Christmastime, and neither should you! Simply combine a variety of dry pet foods with dog or cat treats to make doggone good or "purr-fectly" delicious snack mixes. Packaged in clear bags, the gifts are presented with new pet toys and food dishes that are festively decorated with paint pens.

FAVORITE PETS' SNACK MIXES

DOG SNACK MIX

Combine a variety of dry dog food and dog treats to yield 6 cups. Store in an airtight container.

CAT SNACK MIX

Combine a variety of dry cat food and cat treats to yield 6 cups. Store in an airtight container.

CHOCOLATE-PEANUT BUTTER DUET

*P*resented in this merry "music" box, a gift of Chocolate-Peanut Butter Bars will help you sing the praises of your choir director! A duet of favorite flavors harmonizes to create the moist, delicious treats, which begin with a packaged cake mix. For delivery, the bars are nestled in a gold box that's topped with a fabric-covered lid. Shimmering gold ribbon and a "notable" ornament are added as a festive grand finale.

CHOCOLATE-PEANUT BUTTER BARS

- 1 package (18.25 ounces) chocolate cake mix
- $1/4$ cup vegetable oil
- $1/4$ cup smooth peanut butter
- $1/4$ cup water
- 1 egg
- 1 teaspoon vanilla extract
- 1 cup sugar
- $1/3$ cup butter or margarine
- $1/3$ cup milk
- 1 cup peanut butter chips
- 1 cup chopped lightly salted peanuts

Preheat oven to 350 degrees. In a medium bowl, combine cake mix, oil, peanut butter, water, egg, and vanilla. Spread mixture into bottom of a 9 x 13-inch baking pan lined with lightly greased waxed paper. Bake 20 to 25 minutes or until edges are lightly browned.

In a heavy medium saucepan, combine sugar, butter, and milk. Stirring constantly, bring mixture to a boil over medium-high

heat; boil 1 minute. Remove from heat and add peanut butter chips; stir until smooth. Stir in peanuts. Spread hot topping over warm baked mixture. Cool 2 hours in pan or until firm enough to cut. Cut into 1 x 2-inch bars. Store in an airtight container.

Yield: about 4 dozen bars

MERRY NOTE BOX

You will need an approx. $7^{1/2}$" dia. papier-mâché box, music-motif fabric to cover lid, sheer gold ribbon same width as side of lid and black gimp trim slightly narrower than side of lid for trim, $1^{1/2}$ yds of $1^{1/2}$"w sheer gold ribbon for bow, metallic gold spray paint, a music-motif ornament, and glue.

1. Spray paint outside of box gold.
2. To cover lid, draw around lid on wrong side of fabric. Cut out fabric about $1/2$" outside pencil line. At about $1/2$" intervals, clip edge of fabric to $1/8$" from line. Center fabric piece right side up on lid. Glue clipped edges of fabric to side of lid. If necessary, trim edges of fabric even with bottom edge of lid.
3. Overlapping ends about $1/2$", glue ribbon same width as side of lid and gimp trim to side of lid.
4. Place gift in box. Tie remaining ribbon around box. Tie ribbon ends into a bow around ornament; trim ends.

QUICK COBBLER KIT

*O*ur no-fuss Cranberry-
Peach Cobbler kit is perfect
for someone who loves home-
style tastes, but without all the
effort! The real secret behind
this quick-to-make recipe is
in the buttery cobbler mix —
it's prepared with packaged
cake mix, spices, and pecans.
Present the mix in a decorated
basket along with canned pie
filling, cranberry sauce, and
the easy baking instructions.

CRANBERRY-PEACH COBBLER

> 1 package (18.25 ounces) yellow
>   cake mix
> 1/2 cup butter or margarine
> 1/2 teaspoon ground cinnamon
> 1/4 teaspoon ground nutmeg
> 1/2 cup chopped pecans
> 2 cans (21 ounces each) peach pie
>   filling and 2 cans (16 ounces
>   each) whole berry cranberry
>   sauce

Place cake mix, butter, cinnamon, and
nutmeg in a large food processor; pulse
process until well blended. Stir in pecans.
Divide cobbler mix in half and place in
2 resealable plastic bags. Store in
refrigerator. Give each bag of cobbler mix
with 1 can pie filling, 1 can cranberry
sauce, and serving instructions.

Yield: about 5 cups mix (2 1/2 cups in
each bag)

To serve: Preheat oven to 350 degrees.
Combine pie filling and cranberry sauce
in a lightly greased 9 x 13-inch baking
dish. Sprinkle cobbler mix over fruit

mixture. Bake 45 minutes or until lightly
browned. Serve warm with ice cream.

Yield: about 12 servings

For bag label and tag, follow *Making a
Tag,* page 123.

*T*his Christmas, why not get together with friends for an international open house! Your offering for this festive occasion can be our colorful Mexican Torta. The spicy loaf layers tortillas with mixtures of cream cheese and cilantro, black beans and salsa, and Cheddar cheese and sour cream. A painted terra-cotta saucer is used to make the "Feliz Navidad" dish. What a charming token to leave with the evening's hostess!

MEXICAN TORTA

1 container (8 ounces) soft cream cheese
1 cup fresh cilantro
2 tablespoons chopped green onion
1 jalapeño pepper, seeded and chopped
1 can (15 ounces) black beans, drained
1 tablespoon salsa
2 cloves garlic, minced
1 teaspoon ground cumin
2 cups (8 ounces) finely shredded Cheddar cheese
1/2 cup sour cream
10 flour tortillas (8-inch diameter), divided
4 jars (4 ounces each) whole pimientos, drained and divided
1 container (6 ounces) frozen guacamole, thawed and divided
1 can (2 1/4 ounces) sliced black olives, drained and divided
Fresh cilantro and jalapeño slices to garnish

Process cream cheese, cilantro, green onion, and jalapeño pepper in a food processor until well blended. Transfer to a small bowl; set aside. Process black beans, salsa, garlic, and cumin in a food processor until mixture is smooth. Combine Cheddar cheese and sour cream in a small bowl; stir until well blended.

To assemble torta, cut a piece of cardboard to fit tortilla; cover with plastic wrap. Layer the following on covered cardboard: tortilla, half of Cheddar cheese mixture, tortilla, half of pimientos, tortilla, half of guacamole, tortilla, half of black bean mixture, half of black olives, tortilla, and half of cream cheese mixture. Repeat layers with remaining ingredients. Garnish with cilantro leaves and jalapeño slices. Cover with plastic wrap and store in refrigerator. Cut into wedges to serve.

Yield: about 20 appetizers

"FELIZ NAVIDAD" DISH

You will need an approx. 10 1/2" dia. flowerpot saucer, dark red acrylic spray paint, assorted colors of liquid acrylic paint (we used white, yellow, gold, pink, blue, and green), paintbrushes, non-toxic clear acrylic sealer, tracing paper, graphite transfer paper, and shredded paper to line dish.

1. Spray paint saucer dark red.
2. Use acrylic paint to paint background colors on saucer as desired.
3. Trace "Feliz Navidad," star, and swirl patterns, page 118, onto tracing paper. Use transfer paper to transfer patterns to rim of saucer. Paint designs. Paint dots around designs.
4. Apply 2 to 3 coats of sealer to dish.
5. Line dish with shredded paper.
6. Dish is for decorative use only. Line with a plate when using dish to serve food. Lightly hand wash dish if necessary.

HOLIDAY SPRITZ COOKIES

*T*he simple tree motifs that decorate this paper bag give a hint of the sweet treats tucked inside! A Yuletide tradition from Scandinavia, Holiday Spritz Cookies are rich, buttery bites that melt in your mouth. A cookie press is used to create the tiny tree shapes, which are flecked with colorful non-pareils.

HOLIDAY SPRITZ COOKIES

    1   cup butter, softened
    1   cup sugar
    1   package (3 ounces) cream cheese,
          softened
    1   egg
    1   teaspoon vanilla extract
 2¹/₃   cups all-purpose flour
   ¹/₂   teaspoon baking powder
   ¹/₄   teaspoon salt
    2   tablespoons green non-pareils
    2   tablespoons red non-pareils

Preheat oven to 375 degrees. In a large bowl, combine butter, sugar, cream cheese, egg, and vanilla; beat until smooth. Sift flour, baking powder, and salt into a medium bowl. Add dry ingredients to creamed mixture; beat until well blended. Stir in non-pareils. Spoon dough into a cookie press fitted with a tree disc. Press cookies onto an ungreased baking sheet. Bake 5 to 7 minutes or until bottoms are very lightly browned. Transfer cookies to a wire rack to cool. Store in an airtight container.

Yield: about 8 dozen cookies

FESTIVE BAG

You will need a brown lunch bag, cream acrylic paint, red and green dimensional paint, compressed craft sponge, red and green baby rickrack, jute twine, an 8¹/₂" x 11" piece of parchment paper, red paper, colored pencils, tracing paper, hole punch, and glue.

1. Trace tree pattern, page 118, onto tracing paper; cut out. Use pattern to cut shape from sponge.
2. Lightly dampen sponge shape. Use sponge shape and follow *Sponge Painting*, page 121, to paint cream trees on bag.

3. Use red and green paint to paint dots on trees and wavy lines around trees.
4. Fold top of bag about 1¹/₂" to back. Punch two holes in folded part of bag. Thread a length of twine through holes and knot at front of bag. Cut a length from each color of rickrack. Tie ends of twine on bag around center of rickrack lengths. Tie ends of twine and rickrack lengths together into a bow.
5. For tag, follow *Making a Tag*, page 123, copying tag design onto parchment paper. Punch a hole in tag. Thread 1 twine streamer through hole and knot to secure.

HERBED FOCACCIA KIT

*F*riends who savor the heady aroma of freshly baked bread will love our Herbed Focaccia Kit, which includes dough and topping mixes, olive oil, and baking instructions. For this version of the Italian specialty, the large, flat rounds are drizzled with olive oil and sprinkled with Parmesan cheese and dried rosemary. Brown paper bags are embellished with ribbon, jute, and handwritten tags for a simple presentation.

HERBED FOCACCIA KIT

DOUGH MIX

- 3³/₄ cups all-purpose flour
- ¹/₄ cup freshly grated Parmesan cheese
- 1 package dry yeast
- 1 teaspoon sugar
- 1 tablespoon dried rosemary leaves
- 2 teaspoons dried minced onion
- 1 teaspoon salt
- ¹/₂ teaspoon garlic powder
- ¹/₂ teaspoon ground black pepper

TOPPING MIX

- 2 tablespoons freshly grated Parmesan cheese
- 1 teaspoon dried rosemary leaves
- ¹/₄ teaspoon garlic powder
- Olive oil to give

For dough mix, combine all ingredients in a medium bowl. Store in an airtight container.

For topping mix, combine cheese, rosemary, and garlic powder in a small bowl. Store in an airtight container in refrigerator. Give with a bottle of olive oil and serving instructions.

To serve: In a large bowl, combine dough mix, 1¹/₂ cups very warm water, and 1 tablespoon olive oil; stir until a soft dough forms. Turn dough onto a lightly floured surface. Knead about 5 minutes or until dough becomes smooth and elastic. Cover and allow dough to rest 10 minutes.

Divide dough in half and press each half into a 9-inch-diameter circle on a lightly greased baking sheet. Drizzle each dough circle with about 1 teaspoon olive oil and sprinkle with topping mix. Cover with plastic wrap and let rise in a warm place (80 to 85 degrees) 45 minutes or until almost doubled in size.

Preheat oven to 425 degrees. Make indentations in dough with fingertips. Bake 14 to 18 minutes or until crust is golden brown. Serve warm with olive oil.

Yield: 2 focaccia rounds

83

FRUITY YULETIDE TEA

*C*hilly Yuletide weather is no match for the warming appeal of Fruity Tea Mix! This whimsical gift is prepared with fun-flavored drink mixes and fruit-shaped candies. For a lighthearted delivery, pack the tea in a gift box adorned with candy, greenery, and a cheery ribbon. A hand-lettered label announces your gift.

FRUITY TEA MIX

    1 cup sweetened powdered
        instant tea mix with lemon flavor
 $^1/_2$ cup sugar
    1 package (0.16 ounce)
        unsweetened punch-flavored
        soft drink mix
    1 package (7$^1/_2$ ounces) fruit-
        shaped fruit-flavored candy

In a medium bowl, combine tea, sugar, soft drink mix, and candy. Store in an airtight container. Give with serving instructions.

Yield: about 2 cups mix

To serve: Pour 8 ounces hot or cold water over 2 tablespoons tea mix; stir until well blended.

FRUITY WREATH BOX

You will need an oval papier-mâché box with lid (our box measures about 5" x 6$^1/_2$"), silk greenery, fruit-shaped candy, 1 yd of 1$^1/_2$"w wired ribbon, green paper, black felt-tip calligraphy pen, serrated-cut craft scissors, wire cutters, and glue.

1. Draw around lid on green paper. Use craft scissors to cut out shape about 1" inside drawn line. Use pen to write "Fruity Tea Mix" on shape. Glue shape to center of lid.
2. Glue greenery along edge of lid. Glue candy pieces to greenery.
3. Place gift in box. Place lid on box. Tie ribbon into a bow around lid; trim ends. If necessary, glue ribbon to secure.

SUNFLOWER SNACK MIX

*P*resented in a sponge-painted gift bag, Sunflower Snack Mix is a high-energy treat that's sure to please someone who loves outdoor activities — like building snowmen! The lightly sweet snack has cinnamony cereal, nuts, and raisins baked with a brown sugar and cranberry juice coating. Super-easy to paint, the lively snow fellow has drawn-on features and tiny silk flower "buttons."

SUNFLOWER SNACK MIX

- 4 cups apple-cinnamon-flavored round oat cereal
- 2 cups sunflower kernels
- 2 cups golden raisins
- 2 cups sliced almonds
- $1/2$ cup firmly packed brown sugar
- $1/2$ cup frozen cranberry juice cocktail concentrate, thawed
- $1/4$ cup plus 2 tablespoons vegetable oil

Preheat oven to 250 degrees. In a large roasting pan, combine cereal, sunflower kernels, raisins, and almonds. In a small bowl, combine brown sugar, juice concentrate, and oil; stir until well blended. Pour over cereal mixture; stir until well coated. Bake 1 hour, stirring every 15 minutes. Spread on waxed paper to cool. Store in an airtight container.

Yield: about 10 cups snack mix

SUNFLOWER SNOWMAN BAG

You will need a brown lunch bag, white acrylic paint, compressed craft sponge, 2" dia. silk sunflower, 3 small silk flowers, black and orange felt-tip pens, natural raffia, hole punch, tracing paper, and glue.

1. Trace circle patterns, page 118, separately onto tracing paper; cut out. Use patterns to cut circles from sponge.
2. Use white paint and sponge circles and follow *Sponge Painting*, page 121, to paint snowman on bag.
3. Use black pen to draw eyes, mouth, and arms and to outline snowman. Use orange pen to draw nose.
4. Glue small flowers to snowman.
5. Place gift in bag.
6. Fold top of bag to back. Punch 2 holes in folded part of bag. Thread several lengths of raffia through holes and tie into a bow at front of bag. Glue sunflower to bow.

HEARTY HOLIDAY SOUP

*Y*ou'll warm hearts and
tummies this Christmas with
gifts of Smoked Turkey and
Cheese Soup and a pretty pot
holder. Thick and hearty, the
soup is loaded with meat,
spices, and two kinds of cheese.
Our handy pot holder, crocheted
with double strands of cotton
yarn, is a classic kitchen helper.
Tuck these pleasing presents in
a simple basket and announce
your regards with a hand-
colored tag.

SMOKED TURKEY AND CHEESE SOUP

     4 cans (14.5 ounces each) chicken
          broth
     4 cups chopped smoked turkey
          (about 1¹/₂ pounds)
  1¹/₃ cups chopped onions
     1 can (4.5 ounces) chopped green
          chiles
   ¹/₃ cup finely chopped celery
   ¹/₄ cup vegetable oil
   ¹/₂ cup all-purpose flour
     2 teaspoons ground cumin
   ¹/₈ teaspoon ground red pepper
     2 cups half and half
   ¹/₄ cup chopped fresh cilantro
     2 cups (8 ounces) shredded
          Monterey Jack cheese
     1 cup (4 ounces) shredded sharp
          Cheddar cheese

In a large stockpot, bring chicken
broth to a simmer over medium-low heat;
add turkey. In a large skillet, sauté
onions, green chiles, and celery in oil
over medium heat about 8 minutes or

until vegetables are tender. In a small
bowl, combine flour, cumin, and red
pepper. Stirring constantly, sprinkle flour
mixture over sautéed mixture; cook about
10 minutes or until mixture begins to
brown. Gradually stir in half and half.
Stirring constantly, cook about 3 minutes
or until mixture begins to thicken.

Continuing to stir, add half and half
mixture to chicken broth. Stir in cilantro.
Stirring occasionally, cook over medium-
low heat about 15 minutes. Add cheeses;
stir until cheeses melt. Serve warm or
store in an airtight container in
refrigerator.

Yield: about 12 cups soup

CROCHETED POT HOLDER

SUPPLIES

100% Cotton Worsted Weight Yarn,
  approximately:
    MC (White) – 1 ounce (30 grams,
      50 yards)
    CC (Red) – ³/₄ ounce (20 grams,
      40 yards)
    Crochet hook, size K (6.50mm) *or* size
      needed for gauge

Note: Entire Pot Holder is worked holding
two strands of yarn together.

ABBREVIATIONS:

CC	Contrasting Color
ch(s)	chain(s)
dc	double crochet(s)
FLO	Front Loop(s) Only
MC	Main Color
mm	millimeters
sc	single crochet(s)
slip st	slip stitch
st(s)	stitch(es)

★ – work instructions following ★ as
many *more* times as indicated in
addition to the first time.

GAUGE: In pattern, 6 sts and 6 rows =
  2¹/₂"

With MC, ch 20.
Row 1 (right side): Sc in second ch from
hook and in each ch across: 19 sc.
Row 2: Ch 1, turn; sc in *both* loops of
first sc, ★ sc in FLO of next sc (Fig. 1), sc
in *both* loops of next sc; repeat from ★
across changing to CC in last sc (Fig. 2).

Fig. 1

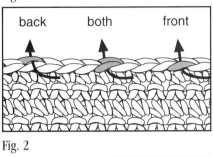

Fig. 2

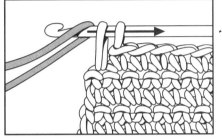

Row 3: Ch 1, turn; sc in *both* loops of
first sc, ★ dc in free loop one row *below*
next sc (Fig. 3), sc in *both* loops of next
sc; repeat from ★ across.

Fig. 3

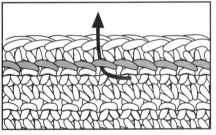

Row 4: Ch 1, turn; sc in *both* loops of
first sc, ★ sc in FLO of next dc, sc in *both*
loops of next sc; repeat from ★ across
changing to MC in last sc.
Row 5: Ch 1, turn; sc in *both* loops of
first sc, ★ dc in free loop one row *below*
next sc, sc in *both* loops of next sc; repeat
from ★ across.

Row 6: Ch 1, turn; sc in *both* loops of
first sc, ★ sc in FLO of next dc, sc in *both*
loops of next sc; repeat from ★ across
changing to CC in last sc.
Rows 7 - 17: Repeat Rows 3 - 6 twice,
then repeat Rows 3 - 5 once *more*.
Row 18: Ch 1, turn; sc in each st across.
Edging: Ch 1, turn; sc in first 18 sc, (2 sc,
ch 10, slip st in side of last sc made, sc)
in last sc; sc evenly across end of rows;
working in free loops of beginning ch
(Fig. 4), 3 sc in first ch, sc in next 17 chs,
3 sc in last ch; sc evenly across end of
rows; 2 sc in same st as first sc; join with
slip st to first sc, finish off.

Fig. 4

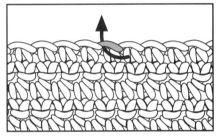

HEARTWARMING TAG

You will need a 3¹/₂" x 5¹/₂" piece of
white card stock paper, tracing paper,
graphite transfer paper, black felt-tip pen,
colored pencils, natural raffia, and a hole
punch.

1. Match short edges and fold paper piece
in half.
2. Trace tag pattern, page 119, onto
tracing paper. Use transfer paper to
transfer pattern to tag. Use pen to draw
over transferred design. Use colored
pencils to color design.
3. Punch a hole in tag and thread a length
of raffia through hole.

SASSY CITRUS VINEGAR

*A*dd a splash of excitement to your seasonal sharing with a gift of tangy Orange-Flavored Vinegar! A fruity infusion of oranges, white wine vinegar, and fresh mint, the condiment can be mixed with a few pantry staples to create Orange-Paprika Dressing. Just a sprinkling of the sassy seasoning makes a simple dinner salad simply delicious! For a gift that looks as wonderful as it tastes, present the vinegar in a wax-sealed bottle adorned with greenery, elegant ribbons, and a handmade tag. Be sure to include the recipe for the dressing, too!

ORANGE-FLAVORED VINEGAR

3 medium oranges
4 cups white wine vinegar
6 fresh mint leaves, rinsed, patted dry, and crushed
    Fresh oranges and wooden skewers to decorate

Peel zest only (orange portion) from oranges. Squeeze juice from oranges and reserve. In a sterilized, dry 2-quart glass container, combine orange zest, orange juice, and vinegar. Add mint leaves. Cover and store in a cool place 2 weeks to allow flavors to develop.

Strain vinegar through several layers of cheesecloth into a 2-quart pitcher. Pour into decorative bottles. Use a vegetable peeler to cut orange zest spirals; thread onto a wooden skewer. Place in bottles of vinegar to decorate. Store in a cool place. Give with recipe for Orange-Paprika Dressing.

Yield: about 4³/₄ cups vinegar

ORANGE-PAPRIKA DRESSING

¹/₂ cup Orange-Flavored Vinegar
¹/₄ cup vegetable oil
1 tablespoon sugar
¹/₂ teaspoon salt
¹/₄ teaspoon paprika
¹/₈ teaspoon ground white pepper

In a small bowl, combine vinegar, oil, sugar, salt, paprika, and white pepper; whisk until well blended. Serve with mixed green salad.

Yield: about ³/₄ cup dressing

DECORATIVE BOTTLE

You will need a decorative bottle with cork (our bottle measures about 11" high), either pearl white Candle Magic® wax crystals or paraffin, 1 yd each of 1¹/₂"w white and green sheer ribbon, 1 yd of 2"w wired gold ribbon, silk greenery, large can for melting wax, a pan to hold can, plastic plate, cooking spray, alcohol, glass cleaner, craft knife, newspaper, 7" of ¹/₁₆" dia. gold cord, hole punch, copier paper, desired color paper for tag, black felt-tip pen, and glue.

1. Refer to recipe to fill bottle with vinegar. Insert cork firmly in bottle.
2. (*Caution:* When melting wax, do not place can directly on burner.) Cover work area with newspaper. Place can in pan on stove (or in electric frying pan); fill pan half full with water. Melt wax crystals or paraffin in can.
3. Spray bottom ²/₃ of bottle with cooking spray to prevent wax from sticking. Place bottle on plate and slowly pour wax over top of bottle. Allowing wax to harden between coats, continue pouring wax over bottle until wax is desired thickness.
4. Use craft knife to cut away unwanted wax on bottle, leaving some drips along bottom edge of wax. Use alcohol to remove wax residue from bottle. Clean uncovered part of bottle with glass cleaner.
5. Tie ribbon lengths together into a bow around neck of bottle; trim ends. Tuck greenery behind bow.
6. For tag, follow *Making a Tag*, page 123. Punch hole in tag and loop cord through hole. Knot ends of cord together. Hang tag on greenery on bottle.

YUMMY PEANUT BUTTER FUDGE

*K*ids will really enjoy giving — and receiving — our yummy Peanut Butter Fudge! They'll also like the idea of decorating the gift boxes with "recycled" Christmas cards. While Mom or Dad prepares the fudge, the youngsters can craft personalized containers using papier-mâché boxes, ribbon, buttons, and glue.

PEANUT BUTTER FUDGE

  2 cups granulated sugar
  1 cup firmly packed brown sugar
  2 cans (5 ounces each) evaporated
     milk
$^{1}/_{2}$ cup butter or margarine
$1^{1}/_{4}$ cups crunchy peanut butter
  1 jar (7 ounces) marshmallow
     creme
  1 teaspoon vanilla extract

Line a 9-inch square baking pan with aluminum foil, extending foil over 2 sides of pan; grease foil. Butter sides of a very heavy large saucepan. Combine sugars, evaporated milk, and butter in saucepan. Stirring constantly, cook over medium-low heat until sugar dissolves. Using a pastry brush dipped in hot water, wash down any sugar crystals on sides of pan. Attach a candy thermometer to pan, making sure thermometer does not touch bottom of pan. Increase heat to medium and bring to a boil. Cook, stirring occasionally, until mixture reaches soft-ball stage (approximately 234 to 240 degrees). Test about $^{1}/_{2}$ teaspoon mixture in ice water. Mixture will easily form a ball in ice water but will flatten when held in your hand. Remove from heat and stir in peanut butter, marshmallow creme, and vanilla. Pour into prepared pan. Cool completely. Chill at least 4 hours or until firm.

Cut into 1-inch squares. Store in an airtight container in a cool place.

Yield: about 4 dozen pieces fudge

CHRISTMAS CARD BOXES

For each box, you will need a papier-mâché box with removable lid insert (we used 3⅝" x 5¼", 4⅝" x 6⅛", and 5¾" x 7¼" boxes), Christmas card to fit in box lid, ⅜"w grosgrain ribbon, assorted buttons, and glue.

1. Remove insert from box lid. Trimming card to fit if necessary, glue card to insert. Replace insert in lid.
2. Glue lengths of ribbon to top of lid. Glue buttons over ribbon ends at corners.

SPLENDID LEMON STARS

Luscious Lemon Star Cookies make splendid gifts for friends who brighten your life through the year! The sugar cookies have a tangy candy center and a tender-crisp texture that's sure to please. A star-shaped paper tag is an easy way to personalize a store-bought bag.

LEMON STAR COOKIES

COOKIES
- 3/4 cup butter or margarine, softened
- 1 cup sugar
- 2 eggs
- 1 teaspoon lemon extract
- 3 cups all-purpose flour
- 1/2 teaspoon baking powder
- 1/2 teaspoon salt

CANDY
- 2/3 cup sugar
- 1/2 cup water
- 2 tablespoons light corn syrup
- 1/2 teaspoon white vinegar
- 1/8 teaspoon salt
- 1/2 teaspoon lemon extract
- 7 drops yellow liquid food coloring

For cookies, cream butter and sugar in a large bowl until fluffy. Add eggs and lemon extract; beat until smooth. In a medium bowl, combine flour, baking powder, and salt. Add dry ingredients to creamed mixture; stir until a soft dough forms. Divide dough into fourths. Wrap in plastic wrap and chill 1 hour.

Preheat oven to 350 degrees. On a lightly floured surface, use a floured rolling pin to roll out one fourth of dough to 1/8-inch thickness. Use a 3-inch star-shaped cookie cutter to cut out cookies. Transfer to a baking sheet lined with lightly greased aluminum foil. Use a 1 1/4-inch star-shaped cookie cutter to cut out star from center of each cookie. Bake 8 to 10 minutes or until cookies are firm. Allow cookies to cool slightly. Transfer cookies on foil to a wire rack; cool completely. Repeat with remaining dough.

For candy, combine sugar, water, corn syrup, vinegar, and salt in a heavy small saucepan. Stirring constantly, cook over medium heat until sugar dissolves. Using a pastry brush dipped in hot water, wash down any sugar crystals on sides of pan.

Attach a candy thermometer to pan, making sure thermometer does not touch bottom of pan. Increase heat to medium-high and bring to a boil. Cook, without stirring, until mixture reaches 270 degrees. Test about 1/2 teaspoon mixture in ice water. Mixture will form hard threads in ice water but will soften when removed from the water. Remove from heat; add lemon extract and tint yellow. (Return saucepan to very low heat as necessary to keep candy melted.) Spoon about 1/4 teaspoonful candy into cutout of each cookie; use a toothpick to pull candy into points of star. Let candy harden; remove cookies from foil. Store cookies in an airtight container.

Yield: about 5 dozen cookies

VEGETARIAN ZUCCHINI LASAGNA

*D*eliver our Vegetarian
Zucchini Lasagna and say
"Ciao!" to a family who enjoys
feasting on Italian cuisine.
Layered with garden-fresh
ingredients and four types of
cheese, the ready-to-bake dish
is created using sliced zucchini
in place of pasta. The recipe
makes enough for two dishes,
so you can treat your own
family, too. For a festive wrap,
present the hearty casserole
in an easy-to-stitch cozy along
with serving directions.

VEGETARIAN ZUCCHINI LASAGNA

SAUCE

- 1½ cups chopped onions
- 2 ribs celery, finely chopped
- 2 cloves garlic, minced
- ¼ cup olive oil
- 2 cans (28 ounces each) Italian plum tomatoes
- 1 can (6 ounces) tomato paste
- 8 ounces fresh mushrooms, thinly sliced
- 1¼ cups shredded carrots
- 1 green pepper, finely chopped
- ¼ cup chopped fresh parsley
- 1 tablespoon sugar
- 1½ teaspoons dried basil leaves
- 1½ teaspoons dried oregano leaves
- ½ teaspoon salt
- ¼ teaspoon ground black pepper
- 1 bay leaf

FILLING

- 4 medium unpeeled zucchini
- 2 containers (15 ounces each) part-skim ricotta cheese
- 2 cups (8 ounces) shredded mozzarella cheese
- 1 cup (4 ounces) freshly grated Parmesan cheese
- ½ cup shredded provolone cheese
- 2 eggs, beaten
- ¼ teaspoon salt
- ⅛ teaspoon ground white pepper

For sauce, sauté onions, celery, and garlic in oil in a Dutch oven over medium heat about 10 minutes or until vegetables are tender. Stir in tomatoes, tomato paste, mushrooms, carrots, green pepper, parsley, sugar, basil, oregano, salt, pepper, and bay leaf. Bring sauce to a simmer. Reduce heat to medium-low. Stirring occasionally, simmer sauce uncovered about 1 hour or until thickened. Remove bay leaf.

For filling, thinly slice zucchini lengthwise. In a large bowl, combine cheeses, eggs, salt, and white pepper; stir until well blended.

Spoon 2 cups sauce into bottom of each of 2 greased 9 x 13-inch baking pans. Add a layer of zucchini slices. In each baking pan, spoon 2 cups cheese mixture over zucchini. Layer again with zucchini, sauce, and remaining cheese mixture. Cover and store in refrigerator. Give with serving instructions.

Yield: 2 casseroles, about 8 servings each

To serve: Uncover lasagna and bake in a 350-degree oven 50 to 60 minutes or until heated through and cheese begins to brown. Remove from oven and allow to stand 10 minutes. Serve warm.

CASSEROLE COZY

For a cozy to fit a 9" x 13" pan, you will need two 14½" x 18½" fabric pieces, a 14½" x 18½" piece of polyester bonded batting, ⅞ yd of ¼"w grosgrain ribbon, and thread to match fabric.

1. Place fabric pieces right sides together; place batting piece on fabric pieces. Using a ½" seam allowance and leaving an opening for turning, sew layers together. Clip seam allowance at corners, turn right side out, and press; sew final closure by hand.

2. For each corner, match edges and fold corner diagonally. Stitch 2¼" from point (Fig. 1).

Fig. 1

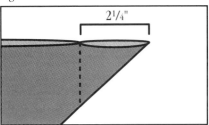

3. For bows, cut ribbon into 4 equal lengths. Tie each length into a bow; trim ends. Hand sew bows to corners of cozy.

CRUNCH-TOP GINGER CAKES

*M*iniature Crunch-Top Ginger Cakes feature a yummy mix of tastes and textures. The spicy sweets are individually wrapped and presented with cute gingerbread boy pins.

CRUNCH-TOP GINGER CAKES

TOPPING

- $^2/_3$ cup chopped pecans, toasted
- $^2/_3$ cup flaked coconut, toasted
- $^1/_4$ cup firmly packed brown sugar
- 3 tablespoons butter or margarine, melted

CAKE

- 3 tablespoons butter or margarine, softened
- $^1/_3$ cup sugar
- $^1/_3$ cup sour cream
- $^1/_3$ cup molasses
- 2 eggs
- 3 tablespoons hot, strongly brewed coffee
- $^1/_2$ teaspoon vanilla extract
- $^1/_4$ teaspoon orange extract
- 1 cup plus 3 tablespoons all-purpose flour
- $^3/_4$ teaspoon baking soda
- $^3/_4$ teaspoon ground cinnamon
- $^3/_4$ teaspoon ground ginger
- $^1/_4$ teaspoon ground allspice
- $^1/_4$ teaspoon salt

Preheat oven to 325 degrees. Heavily grease each mold of a 6-mold fluted tube pan. For topping, process pecans, coconut, brown sugar, and butter in a food processor until nuts and coconut are coarsely ground. Press about 3 tablespoons topping into bottom of each prepared mold.

For cake, cream butter and sugar in a large bowl. Add sour cream, molasses, eggs, coffee, and extracts; beat until smooth. In a small bowl, combine flour, baking soda, cinnamon, ginger, allspice, and salt. Add dry ingredients to creamed mixture; stir until well blended. Spoon about $^1/_3$ cup batter into each mold. Bake 17 to 22 minutes or until a toothpick inserted in center of cake comes out clean. Cool in pan 30 minutes. Invert cakes onto a wire rack and cool completely.

Yield: 6 small cakes

GINGERBREAD BOY PINS

For each pin, you will need brown fabric; ivory felt; muslin; fusible web; 6" of $^1/_8$"w green ribbon; white baby rickrack; white, red, green, and black acrylic paint; small paintbrushes; a pin back; and glue.

1. Fuse web to muslin. Fuse muslin to 1 side (back) of felt.
2. Use gingerbread boy pattern, page 119, and follow *Making Appliqués*, page 121, to make 1 gingerbread boy from brown fabric. Fuse gingerbread boy to front of felt. Cutting close to shape, cut gingerbread boy from felt.
3. Paint black eyes, red mouth, green buttons, and white stitches on gingerbread boy.
4. Glue lengths of rickrack to gingerbread boy.
5. Tie ribbon into a bow; trim ends. Glue bow to gingerbread boy.
6. Glue pin back to back of gingerbread boy.

SPICY CHRISTMAS HEARTS

A dusting of sugar gives our Spicy Christmas Hearts wintry appeal! The cutout cookies, made with molasses, cinnamon, and cloves, have a wonderful holiday aroma and tummy-pleasing taste. For a presentation that reflects your warmest wishes, deliver the treats in a crafty gift bag accented with no-sew heart appliqués.

SPICY CHRISTMAS HEARTS

- 3/4 cup butter or margarine, softened
- 1/3 cup firmly packed brown sugar
- 1/3 cup granulated sugar
- 1 cup molasses
- 3 1/2 cups all-purpose flour
- 3/4 teaspoon baking soda
- 3/4 teaspoon ground cinnamon
- 3/4 teaspoon ground cloves
- 1/4 teaspoon salt
- Granulated sugar to decorate

In a large bowl, cream butter, brown sugar, and 1/3 cup granulated sugar until fluffy. Add molasses; beat until smooth. In a medium bowl, combine flour, baking soda, cinnamon, cloves, and salt. Gradually add dry ingredients to creamed mixture; stir until a soft dough forms. Divide dough into fourths. Wrap in plastic wrap and chill 8 hours or overnight.

Preheat oven to 350 degrees. On a lightly floured surface, use a floured rolling pin to roll out one fourth of dough to 1/8-inch thickness. Use a 2 1/4-inch-wide heart-shaped cookie cutter to cut out cookies. Transfer to a greased baking sheet. Sprinkle cookies with granulated

sugar. Bake 6 to 8 minutes or until edges are lightly browned. Transfer cookies to a wire rack to cool. Repeat with remaining dough. Store in an airtight container.

Yield: about 10 dozen cookies

HEART APPLIQUÉ BAG

You will need a brown lunch bag, 2 fabrics for appliqués and trim at top of bag, fusible web, a button, black felt-tip pen, and glue.

1. Use heart patterns, page 119, and follow *Making Appliqués*, page 121, to make hearts.
2. Fuse hearts to center front of bag. Glue button to hearts.

3. For bow, cut a 3/4" x 10" strip from 1 fabric. Tie strip into a bow, trim ends, and set aside.
4. For remaining trim at top of bag, fuse web to wrong sides of fabrics. Cut a 1/2" x 6" strip from bow fabric; cut strip into eight 3/4" long pieces. Measure around top of bag; add 1/2". Cut a 1 1/4"w strip the determined measurement from remaining fabric.
5. Fuse wide fabric strip around bag about 3/4" from top. Glue bow to center of strip. Spacing evenly, fuse remaining fabric pieces along center of strip.
6. Use pen to draw stitches around appliqués and trim on bag.

Holiday Pizza

READY-TO-COOK HOLIDAY PIZZA

*A*n after-caroling party is the perfect place to deliver this savory surprise. Topped with a harmonious combination of Italian sausage, veggies, and cheese, our Ready-to-Cook Holiday Pizza will make taste buds sing! For a noteworthy presentation, a take-out pizza box is dressed up with fused-on fabric and tied with a jute bow. You can cue the host that this treat is for immediate enjoyment by writing the serving instructions on the gift tag.

1 package dry yeast
1/2 teaspoon sugar
1 1/2 cups warm water
2 tablespoons vegetable oil
2 to 2 1/4 cups all-purpose flour, divided
1 1/2 cups whole-wheat flour
1 teaspoon salt
1 pound Italian sausage
1/2 cup prepared pizza sauce, divided
2 cups (8 ounces) shredded Mozzarella cheese, divided
1 jar (2.5 ounces) sliced mushrooms, drained and divided
1 can (2.25 ounces) sliced black olives, drained and divided
Sweet red pepper, green pepper, and yellow pepper to decorate

In a small bowl, dissolve yeast and sugar in 1 1/2 cups warm water. Stir oil into yeast mixture. In a medium bowl, combine 1 1/2 cups all-purpose flour, whole-wheat flour, and salt. Add yeast mixture to dry ingredients; stir until a soft dough forms. Turn onto a lightly floured surface and knead 5 minutes or until dough becomes smooth and elastic, using additional flour as necessary. Cover and let dough rest 10 minutes. Divide dough in half and press into 2 lightly greased 12-inch pizza pans. Cover and let rise in a warm place (80 to 85 degrees) 30 minutes.

Preheat oven to 425 degrees. Bake crusts 7 minutes or just until dry. Place on a wire rack to cool.

In a medium skillet, brown sausage; drain, crumble, and set aside. Transfer cooled crusts to 12-inch-diameter cardboard circles. Spread half of pizza sauce over each crust. Layer each pizza with half of sausage, cheese, mushrooms, and olives. Slice red and green peppers into rings. Use a 3/4-inch- and a 1 1/2-inch-wide star-shaped cookie cutter to cut out yellow pepper stars. Place pepper pieces on pizzas. Cover tightly with plastic wrap. Store in refrigerator. Give with serving instructions.

Yield: two 12-inch pizzas, about 8 servings each

To serve: Preheat oven to 425 degrees. Remove plastic wrap and slide pizza off cardboard onto a pizza pan or baking sheet. Bake 22 to 25 minutes or until heated through and cheese melts.

FABRIC-COVERED PIZZA BOX

You will need an approx. 13" pizza take-out box, Christmas-motif fabric, fusible web, jute twine, tan and red paper, black felt-tip pen, decorative-edge craft scissors (optional), and glue.

1. Fuse web to wrong side of fabric.
2. Cut a piece of fabric large enough to cover pizza company name on top of box. Fuse fabric piece to box. Repeat for sides of box.
3. Place pizza in box. Tie twine into a bow around box.
4. For tag, either tear or use craft scissors to cut a piece of tan paper. Use pen to write serving instructions on tag. Glue tag to red paper. Cutting close to tag, cut tag from red paper.

GREEK CHEESE SPREAD

*L*end international flavor to gift-giving with a basket packed with creamy Greek Cheese Spread and crackers. The savory blend features tangy feta cheese, rich Kalamata olives, and toasted sesame seeds.

GREEK CHEESE SPREAD

- 2 packages (8 ounces each) cream cheese, softened
- 1 package (8 ounces) feta cheese, crumbled
- 2 tablespoons chopped fresh parsley
- 1 tablespoon freshly squeezed lemon juice
- 1 clove garlic, minced
- 1/2 teaspoon dried oregano leaves
- 1/4 teaspoon ground black pepper
- 1/3 cup pitted and chopped Kalamata olives
- 2 tablespoons sesame seed, toasted
  Crackers to serve

Process cream cheese, feta cheese, parsley, lemon juice, garlic, oregano, and black pepper in a food processor until well blended. Add olives; pulse process just until blended. Spoon into a serving container. Sprinkle with sesame seed. Cover and store in refrigerator. Serve with crackers.

Yield: about 3 cups cheese spread

JOLLY SNOWMEN GIFT BASKET

You will need a small basket, snowman-motif fabric, checked fabric to coordinate with snowman fabric, and fusible web. *For tag,* you will *also* need 1/8"w ribbon, white paper, and a hole punch.

BASKET LINER
Tear a piece of snowman-motif fabric to line basket. Tear a slightly larger piece from checked fabric. Center snowman-motif fabric on checked fabric. Place liner in basket.

NAPKINS
1. Tear one 9" square from checked fabric for each napkin. Fringe edges about 1/4".
2. Fuse web to wrong side of snowman-motif fabric. Cutting close to motifs, cut 1 motif from fabric for each napkin.
3. Fuse 1 motif to 1 corner of each napkin.

TAG
1. For tag background, fuse web to wrong side of checked fabric. Fuse fabric to white paper.
2. Fuse web to wrong sides of snowman-motif fabric and a second piece of white paper.
3. Cut a motif from snowman-motif fabric. Cut a rectangle from white paper slightly taller than snowman motif and wide enough for message.
4. Fuse white paper piece and snowman motif to tag background.
5. Cutting close to motif and paper, cut out tag. Punch a hole in tag. Loop ribbon through hole.

LUSCIOUS LEMON-NUT BREAD

*S*hare this moist, nutty loaf with your best coffee-break pal. Packed with homemade goodness, Lemon-Nut Bread is easy to make with items you probably have on hand. While the bread is baking, you can whip up a cheery no-sew gift bag and matching tag using cute print fabric and fusible web.

LEMON-NUT BREAD

$^3/_4$ cup butter or margarine, softened
$1^1/_2$ cups sugar
3 eggs
$2^1/_4$ cups all-purpose flour
$^1/_4$ teaspoon salt
$^1/_4$ teaspoon baking soda
$^1/_4$ cup buttermilk
$^3/_4$ cup chopped pecans
Grated zest of 1 lemon
$^3/_4$ cup sifted confectioners sugar
6 tablespoons freshly squeezed lemon juice

Preheat oven to 325 degrees. Grease and flour a 5 x 9-inch loaf pan. In a large bowl, cream butter and sugar until fluffy. Add eggs; beat until smooth. In a medium bowl, combine flour, salt, and baking soda. Alternately add dry ingredients and buttermilk to creamed mixture; stir just until moistened. Stir in pecans and lemon zest. Spoon batter into prepared pan. Bake $1^1/_4$ hours or until a toothpick inserted in center of loaf comes out clean. Cool in pan 15 minutes. Remove from pan and place on a wire rack with waxed paper underneath. In a small bowl, combine confectioners sugar and lemon juice. Use a toothpick to punch holes in

top of warm bread; pour glaze over bread. Cool bread completely. Store in an airtight container.

Yield: 1 loaf bread

SNOWMAN FABRIC BAG AND TAG

You will need snowman-motif fabric, $^3/_4$ yd of $^7/_8$"w wired ribbon, $^3/_8$ yd of $^1/_{16}$"w ribbon, $^1/_2$"w fusible web tape, fusible web, poster board, tracing paper, and hole punch.

1. For bag, cut a $9^1/_2$" x 35" fabric piece. Match right sides and short edges and press fabric piece in half (fold is bottom of bag). Unfold fabric piece and fuse web

tape along each long edge on right side. Refold fabric piece and fuse edges together. Fold top of bag 2" to wrong side and press. Unfold top of bag and fuse web tape along top edge on wrong side. Refold top of bag and fuse in place. Turn bag right side out.

2. Place gift in bag. Tie $^7/_8$"w ribbon into a bow around top of bag; trim ends.

3. For tag, cut a 3" square from fabric with desired motif at center. Fuse web to wrong side of fabric. Fuse fabric to poster board. Trace circle pattern, page 119, onto tracing paper; cut out. Use pattern to cut tag from fabric-covered poster board. Punch hole in tag. Loop remaining ribbon through hole in tag. Tie tag onto bow on bag.

CHRISTMASY CONDIMENTS

*T*hese home-style recipes make lots of little gifts for club members or other groups. Crunchy Celery Relish, packed with tangy ingredients, is delicious with beef, pork, or poultry. The spicy sweetness of Cranberry Chutney is also tasty served with meats, as well as breads and cheese. Spruce up the jar lids and basket by covering them with country-look fabrics.

CRUNCHY CELERY RELISH

   3 cups celery, chopped
   1 cup green pepper, chopped
   1 cup red pepper, chopped
   1 cup unpeeled and chopped
        Granny Smith apple
 $^1/_2$ cup onion, chopped
   1 clove garlic, minced
 $^1/_2$ cup apple cider vinegar
 $^1/_4$ cup sugar
   2 tablespoons prepared mustard
 $^1/_2$ teaspoon salt
 $^1/_2$ teaspoon celery seed
 $^1/_2$ teaspoon mustard seed
 $^1/_4$ teaspoon ground white pepper
 $^1/_4$ teaspoon ground allspice

Combine celery, green and red peppers, apple, onion, and garlic in a heat-resistant medium bowl; toss gently. Set aside. In a small saucepan, combine remaining ingredients. Whisking constantly, cook over medium heat about 5 minutes or until heated through. Pour over vegetable mixture; toss gently to coat. Spoon into heat-resistant jars; cool to room temperature. Chill 8 hours to allow flavors to blend. Store in refrigerator.

Yield: about 6 cups relish

CRANBERRY CHUTNEY

   1 pound fresh cranberries
   1 cup granulated sugar
 $^1/_2$ cup firmly packed brown sugar
 $^1/_2$ cup golden raisins
   2 teaspoons ground cinnamon
 $1^1/_2$ teaspoons ground ginger
 $^1/_2$ teaspoon ground cloves
 $^1/_4$ teaspoon ground allspice
   1 cup water
   1 cup chopped onion
   1 cup unpeeled and chopped apple
 $^1/_2$ cup chopped celery

In a Dutch oven, combine cranberries, sugars, raisins, cinnamon, ginger, cloves, allspice, and water. Stirring frequently, cook uncovered over medium-high heat about 15 minutes or until juice is released from cranberries. Stir in remaining ingredients. Reduce heat to low. Stirring occasionally, simmer until thickened. Spoon into heat-resistant jars; cover and cool to room temperature. Store in refrigerator up to 2 weeks. Serve chilled.

Yield: about 5 cups chutney

FESTIVE FABRIC-COVERED BASKET

You will need an approx. 7" dia. round basket, 2 coordinating fabrics, fusible web, polyester fiberfill, natural raffia, pinking shears, large rubber band, white poster board, black felt-tip pen, shredded paper to line basket, and glue.

1. Measure basket from 1 side of rim to opposite side of rim (Fig. 1); add 8". Cut a circle from each fabric the determined measurement.

Fig. 1

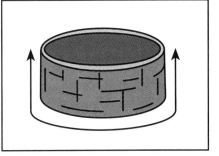

2. Fuse web to wrong side of 1 fabric circle. Fuse circles wrong sides together. Use pinking shears to trim edge of fused circle.
3. Center basket on fabric circle. Place fiberfill around basket for desired fullness. Bring edges of fabric circle up around fiberfill. Place rubber band around fabric circle and basket even with rim of basket. Adjust fabric evenly. If necessary, glue fabric to basket to secure.
4. Knot several lengths of raffia around fabric, covering rubber band; trim ends about 3" from knot. Line basket with shredded paper.
5. For each jar lid, use pinking shears to cut an approx. 6" dia. circle from fabric. Unscrew band from jar, center fabric circle over lid, and replace band.
6. For tag, follow *Making a Fabric-Backed Tag*, page 123. Use pen to write message on tag.

TANGY PICKLED EGGS

*H*ere's a unique gift idea for a friend who has "egg-ceptional" tastes! Blushed with color, Beet-Pickled Eggs have a tangy flavor that's sure to wake up a tray of appetizers. To make this exuberant offering extra festive, decorate the container with red and green raffia and a dapper little fellow made from a plastic egg.

BEET-PICKLED EGGS

12	hard-cooked eggs, peeled
1³/₄	cups white vinegar
²/₃	cup beet liquid (drained from a 15-ounce can of beets)
¹/₃	cup dry white wine
8	black peppercorns
3	whole cloves
3	cloves garlic
1	bay leaf
1	tablespoon sugar
¹/₂	teaspoon salt
¹/₈	teaspoon ground allspice
2	sprigs fresh dill weed

Place eggs in a 2-quart heat-resistant jar. In a large saucepan combine vinegar, beet liquid, white wine, peppercorns, cloves, garlic, bay leaf, sugar, salt, and allspice. Bring mixture to a boil over medium-high heat. Reduce heat to low; simmer 3 minutes. Pour hot mixture over eggs; add dill weed. Cover and store in refrigerator 2 days to let flavors blend. Store in refrigerator up to 1 week.

Yield: 12 servings

102

CRIMSON RASPBERRY SAUCE

*G*ive a gift of Crimson Raspberry Sauce and help a harried holiday hostess transform ordinary desserts into extraordinary treats! The topping is an easy-to-make complement for cheesecake, ice cream, fruit, and more. A ready-made berry basket and a bit of ribbon are all it takes to wrap up this sweet surprise.

CRIMSON RASPBERRY SAUCE

    1/4 cup sugar
  1 1/2 teaspoons cornstarch
      1 package (10 ounces) frozen red
         raspberries, thawed and drained
    1/2 cup red currant jelly

In a small bowl, combine sugar and cornstarch. In a medium saucepan, combine raspberries and jelly. Stirring frequently, cook over medium-high heat until jelly melts. Stir in sugar mixture and bring to a boil. Reduce heat to medium. Stirring constantly, cook 3 minutes or until liquid is clear and thick. Press through a sieve or food mill. Store in an airtight container in refrigerator. Serve chilled.

Yield: about 1 cup sauce

CRANBERRY-NUT MUFFINS

Take a batch of fruity Cranberry-Nut Muffins to a mom who's too busy for holiday baking. She's sure to appreciate the moist homemade treats, especially when they're spread with lightly sweet Orange Butter. A basket lined with holiday fabric makes a cheery presentation, and a handmade gift tag lends a personal touch.

CRANBERRY-NUT MUFFINS WITH ORANGE BUTTER

MUFFINS

    2   cups all-purpose flour
    2/3 cup sugar
    2   teaspoons baking powder
    1   teaspoon salt
    1/2 teaspoon baking soda
    1/2 teaspoon ground cinnamon
    1/2 cup orange juice
    1/2 cup orange marmalade
    1/4 cup buttermilk
    1/4 cup vegetable oil
    1   egg
    1   cup coarsely chopped fresh
        cranberries
    3/4 cup chopped walnuts

ORANGE BUTTER

    1/2 cup butter, softened
    2   tablespoons orange marmalade

Preheat oven to 375 degrees. For muffins, combine flour, sugar, baking powder, salt, baking soda, and cinnamon in a large bowl. In a small bowl, combine orange juice, orange marmalade,

buttermilk, oil, and egg. Make a well in center of dry ingredients. Add orange juice mixture, cranberries, and walnuts; stir just until moistened. Fill paper-lined muffin cups about two-thirds full. Bake 17 to 22 minutes or until muffins are golden brown. Serve warm or transfer to a wire rack to cool. Store in an airtight container.

For orange butter, combine butter and orange marmalade in a small bowl. Store in an airtight container in refrigerator.

Yield: about 1½ dozen muffins and about ¾ cup orange butter

For gingerbread man tag, trace gingerbread man pattern, page 120, onto tracing paper; cut out. Use pattern to cut shape from tan paper. Use a black felt-tip pen to draw eyes and mouth on gingerbread man and a red colored pencil to color cheeks. Glue gingerbread man to green paper. Cutting close to gingerbread man, cut shape from green paper. Cut a 2½" x 1½" piece of white paper. Glue white paper piece to red paper. Cutting close to white paper piece, cut piece from red paper. Glue to gingerbread man. Use a red pen to write name on tag.

HEARTWARMING DELIGHTS

*E*nchant the ladies in your women's club with gifts of airy Pecan Meringue Cookies. The delicate confections are baked with a generous portion of toasted chopped pecans folded into a vanilla-flavored meringue. Packaged in plastic bags and tied with ribbon, your heartwarming surprises are ready for delivery when tucked in these festive canvas totes. The totes are embellished with fused-on fabric appliqués and heart-shaped paper tags.

PECAN MERINGUE COOKIES

- 1/2 cup firmly packed brown sugar, divided
- 1/2 cup all-purpose flour
- 1/4 teaspoon salt
- 4 egg whites
- 1/2 teaspoon vanilla extract
- 3/4 cup granulated sugar
- 3 cups chopped pecans, toasted

Preheat oven to 325 degrees. In a medium bowl, combine 1/4 cup brown sugar, flour, and salt; set aside. In another medium bowl, beat egg whites until soft peaks form; add vanilla. Gradually add granulated sugar and remaining 1/4 cup brown sugar; beat until stiff peaks form. Gently fold flour mixture into egg white mixture. Fold in pecans. Drop teaspoonfuls of mixture onto a baking sheet lined with parchment paper. Bake 7 to 9 minutes or until bottoms are lightly browned. Transfer to a wire rack to cool. Store in an airtight container.

Yield: about 8 dozen cookies

CHRISTMAS TOTES

For each tote, you will need a 4¹/₂" x 6" canvas tote, fabric for background, Christmas-motif fabric for appliqué, fusible web, 6" of ¹/₈"w and ¹/₃ yd of ³/₈"w ribbon, cream and a second color of paper, black felt-tip pen, tracing paper, and a hole punch.

1. Fuse web to wrong sides of fabrics and cream paper.
2. Cut a 3¹/₂" x 4¹/₂" piece from background fabric. Center and fuse fabric piece to front of tote.
3. Cut a motif from appliqué fabric. Center and fuse motif to background fabric. (Our appliqué fabric has printed blanket stitches along edges of motifs. If your fabric does not have printed stitches, use black pen to draw stitches.)
4. For tag, trace heart pattern, page 120, onto tracing paper; cut out. Use pattern to cut heart from cream paper. Fuse heart to remaining paper. Cutting close to heart, cut heart from paper. Use pen to draw stitches and write name on tag.
5. Punch a hole in tag. Thread narrow ribbon through hole and tie tag to handle of tote. Tie wide ribbon into a bow around handle above tag.

PEANUT BUTTER BEARS

*I*f you can't bear the idea of giving ho-hum gifts, then share these tasty teddies inspired by a favorite childhood toy. Kissed with honey and a touch of cinnamon, our bow-tied Peanut Butter Bears will make the holiday brighter for a youngster — and the young at heart! Presented in a napkin-embellished bag, this gift is sweetened with candy canes and a bright red bow.

PEANUT BUTTER BEARS

$3/4$ cup butter or margarine, softened
   1 cup smooth peanut butter
   1 cup firmly packed brown sugar
$3/4$ cup granulated sugar
   2 eggs
   2 tablespoons honey
$2^1/2$ cups all-purpose flour
$1/2$ teaspoon ground cinnamon
$1/2$ teaspoon baking soda
$1/2$ teaspoon baking powder
$1/4$ teaspoon salt
   Semisweet chocolate mini chips, 1 tube (4.25 ounces) chocolate decorating icing, and 1 tube (4.25 ounces) red decorating icing to decorate

Preheat oven to 350 degrees. In a large bowl, cream butter, peanut butter, and sugars; beat until fluffy. Add eggs and honey; beat until smooth. In a medium bowl, combine flour, cinnamon, baking soda, baking powder, and salt. Add dry ingredients to creamed mixture; stir until a soft dough forms. Divide dough into fourths. On a lightly floured surface, use a floured rolling pin to roll out one fourth of dough to $1/8$-inch thickness. Use a $3^1/2$ x 4-inch bear-shaped cookie cutter to cut out cookies. Place 1 inch apart on a greased baking sheet. Press chocolate chips, flat side up, into cookies for eyes and noses. Bake 7 to 10 minutes or until bottoms are lightly browned. Cool cookies on baking sheet 2 minutes; transfer to a wire rack to cool completely. Repeat with remaining dough.

Transfer chocolate icing into a pastry bag fitted with a very small round tip. Pipe ears and mouth onto each bear. Transfer red icing into a pastry bag fitted with a small round tip. Pipe ribbon onto each bear. Allow icing to harden. Store in an airtight container.

Yield: about 3 dozen cookies

SANTA BAG

You will need a white lunch bag, a large printed paper napkin (our napkin measured $6^1/2$" square when folded), $1/2$ yd of $7/8$"w satin ribbon, 2 wrapped candy canes, and spray adhesive.

1. Unfold and press napkin. Separate napkin into layers. Discard all but printed layer of napkin.
2. Use spray adhesive to carefully glue printed napkin layer to front of bag. Trim napkin layer even with edges of bag.
3. Place gift in bag. Fold top of bag about 2" to front for flap. Cut 2 vertical slits close together through flap and bag. Thread ribbon through slits and tie into a bow at front of bag; trim ends. Place candy canes behind bow.

RASPBERRY SWIRL COOKIES

*W*ho wouldn't be thrilled to receive this cute-as-a-button basket filled with delectable Raspberry Swirl Cookies! For irresistible goodness in every bite, the sliced sweets have a nutty raspberry filling rolled in tender sugar cookie dough. To make a charming delivery, we lined an ordinary basket with a square of torn fabric that's embellished with assorted buttons. A coordinating bow and simple tag complete your gift.

RASPBERRY SWIRL COOKIES

COOKIES

- $1/2$ cup butter or margarine, softened
- 1 cup sugar
- 1 egg
- 1 teaspoon vanilla extract
- 2 cups all-purpose flour
- 1 teaspoon baking powder
- $1/4$ teaspoon salt

RASPBERRY FILLING

- $1/2$ cup seedless raspberry jam
- $1/2$ cup flaked coconut
- $1/4$ cup finely chopped walnuts

For cookies, cream butter and sugar in a medium bowl until fluffy. Add egg and vanilla; beat until smooth. In a small bowl, combine flour, baking powder, and salt. Add dry ingredients to creamed mixture; stir until a soft dough forms. Shape dough into a ball. Wrap in plastic wrap and chill 2 hours.

For raspberry filling, combine jam, coconut, and walnuts; stir until well blended. On floured waxed paper, roll dough into a 9 x12-inch rectangle. Spread filling evenly to within $1/2$-inch of edges. Beginning at 1 long edge, carefully roll up dough jellyroll style, peeling waxed paper from dough as you roll. Pinch seam to seal. Wrap roll in plastic wrap and chill 1 hour or until firm.

Preheat oven to 375 degrees. Cut dough into $1/4$-inch slices. Place 2 inches apart on a baking sheet lined with parchment paper. Bake 8 to 10 minutes or until edges are lightly browned. Immediately transfer cookies to a wire rack to cool. Store in an airtight container.

Yield: about 4 dozen cookies

MAPLE PECAN LOGS

*T*o make four fabulous
gifts at once, stir up our Maple
Pecan Logs! Featuring a luscious
nougat-like center, the logs are
covered with rich caramel and
rolled in crispy toasted pecans.
For sharing, each candy log is
wrapped in cellophane and tied
with cheery ribbon bows. The
photocopied gift tag is simply
colored with pencils.

MAPLE PECAN LOGS

  1 package (16 ounces)
      confectioners sugar, sifted
  1 jar (7 ounces) marshmallow creme
  2 teaspoons maple flavoring
1¹/₂ teaspoons vanilla extract
  1 package (14 ounces) caramels
  3 tablespoons water
  2 cups finely chopped pecans, toasted

In a large bowl, combine confectioners
sugar, marshmallow creme, maple
flavoring, and vanilla. Knead mixture on a
flat surface until all sugar is incorporated.
Divide mixture into fourths; shape each
piece into a 5-inch-long roll. Transfer
rolls to a baking sheet. Chill rolls while
melting caramels.

In top of a double boiler, melt caramels
with water over simmering water; stir
until smooth. Remove from heat. Dip each
roll in caramel mixture; roll in pecans.
Chill about 1 hour or until firm. Wrap
each log in plastic wrap. Store in an
airtight container in a cool place.

Yield: 4 pecan logs

For tag, follow *Making a Tag,* page 123.

*H*oliday gift-giving is in the bag with this fun, frosty fellow! The wintry visitor takes shape from our Giant Snowman Cookie Kit, which includes cookie mix and assorted candies to decorate the cookie. Each batch yields enough dough to make four snowmen — and several "snowballs," too! For a cool presentation, pack the supplies in decorated bags and place the sacks, a cookie cutter, and baking instructions in a ribbon-tied basket.

GIANT SNOWMAN COOKIE KIT

- 5 cups all-purpose flour
- 3 1/2 cups sugar
- 2 teaspoons baking powder
- 1 teaspoon salt
- 1 1/2 cups vegetable shortening
  Candy corn, black jelly beans, and cherry string twist licorice to decorate

In a large bowl, combine flour, sugar, baking powder, and salt. Using a pastry blender or 2 knives, cut shortening into dry ingredients until mixture resembles coarse meal. Divide cookie mix in half and place in 2 resealable plastic bags. Store in refrigerator. Give each bag of mix with a 7 inch-wide x 9-inch-high gingerbread boy cookie cutter, cookie decorations, and recipe for Snowman Cookies.

Yield: about 11 cups cookie mix (5 1/2 cups in each bag)

SNOWMAN COOKIES

Cookie Mix (5 1/2 cups)
- 1 egg
- 1/4 cup water
- 1 teaspoon vanilla extract
  Confectioners sugar

Preheat oven to 375 degrees. In a large bowl, combine cookie mix, egg, water, and vanilla; stir until well blended. Shape into a ball. On greased aluminum foil, use a rolling pin dusted with confectioners sugar to roll out dough to 1/4-inch thickness. Transfer foil with dough to baking sheet. Use cookie cutter to cut out cookie; remove dough scraps. Bake 10 to 12 minutes or until bottom is lightly browned. Transfer cookie on foil to a flat surface to decorate. Decorate warm cookie with candies. Use candy corn for nose, jelly bean halves for eyes and buttons, and 3 strings of licorice for scarf. Repeat with remaining dough and candies to make 3 additional snowmen. Allow cookies to cool before removing from foil.

Shape remaining dough into 4 balls; place on a greased baking sheet. Press into 1/4-inch-thick "snowballs." Bake 7 to 9 minutes or until bottoms are lightly browned. Store in an airtight container.

Yield: about 4 large snowman cookies and 4 snowball cookies

COOKIE BASKET

You will need a basket (ours measures about 10" in diameter); an approx. 9"h gingerbread boy cookie cutter; a white lunch bag and 2 small white bags (ours measure 3" x 6 1/2"); 1 5/8"w ribbon to fit around basket; 5/8 yd of 1 1/2"w ribbon for bow; red, blue, and green jumbo and baby rickrack; red and green embroidery floss; red and green buttons; white, red, and green paper; red and black felt-tip pens; white pencil; tracing paper; graphite transfer paper; large needle; and glue.

1. For recipe card, cut a 4" x 6" piece of red paper. Match short edges and fold paper piece in half.
2. Cut a 2 1/2" x 3 1/4" piece of white paper to fit on front of card, a 4 1/4" x 5 1/4" piece of red paper to fit on lunch bag, and a 2 3/8" x 3 1/8" piece of green paper to fit on each small bag. Glue paper pieces to card and bags. Glue lengths of rickrack over edges of paper pieces.
3. Trace "snowman cookie kit," "button up! eyes for you!," "warm clothes! cold nose!," and recipe card patterns, page 120, separately onto tracing paper. Use transfer paper to transfer patterns to card and bags. Use black pen to draw over designs. Use white pencil to draw snowflakes on bags. Use red pen to write names on recipe card. Write recipe in recipe card.
4. Place cookie mix in lunch bag, jelly beans in 1 small bag, and candy corn and licorice in remaining small bag. Fold top of lunch bag about 1 1/4" to back and top of each small bag about 3/4" to back. Use embroidery floss to sew a button at center of folded part of each bag, tying ends of floss at front of button. Trim ends of floss about 1 1/2" from buttons.
5. For basket, measure around outside of basket; add 1". Cut a length of 1 5/8"w ribbon the determined measurement. Overlapping ends, glue ribbon around basket. Tie remaining ribbon into a bow; trim ends. Glue bow to basket. Glue a button to bow.
6. Place bags, cookie cutter, and recipe card in basket.

111

"GINGERBREAD"
BOX

(Page 11)

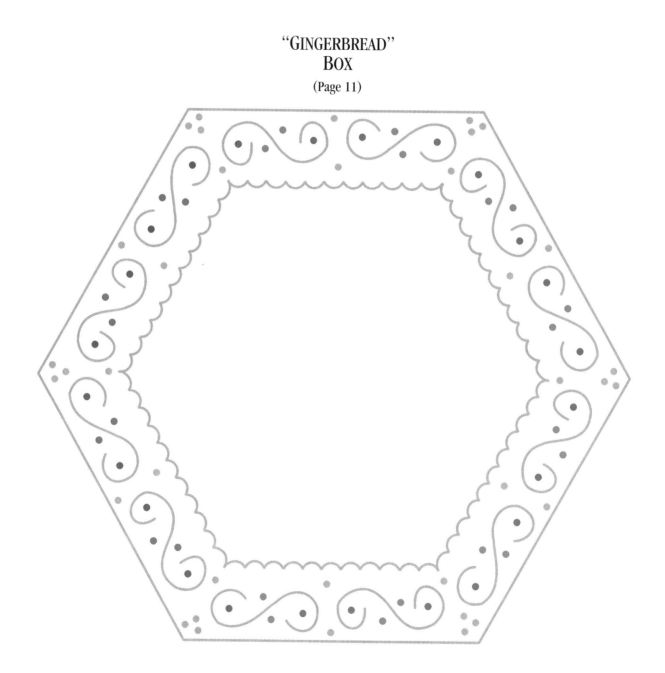

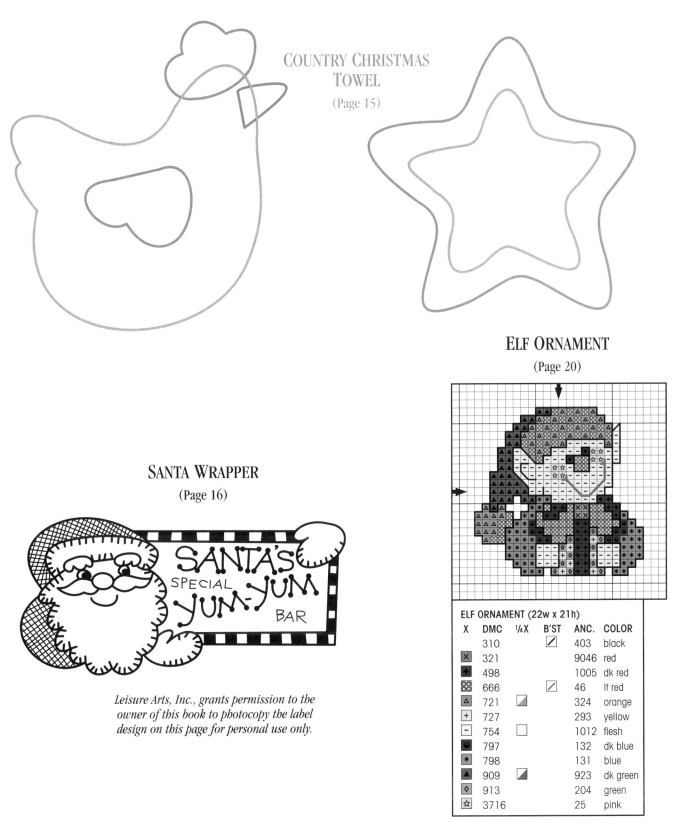

COUNTRY CHRISTMAS TOWEL

(Page 15)

ELF ORNAMENT

(Page 20)

SANTA WRAPPER

(Page 16)

SANTA'S
SPECIAL
YUM-YUM
BAR

Leisure Arts, Inc., grants permission to the owner of this book to photocopy the label design on this page for personal use only.

ELF ORNAMENT (22w x 21h)

X	DMC	¼X	B'ST	ANC.	COLOR
	310		╱	403	black
☒	321			9046	red
◆	498			1005	dk red
▨	666		╱	46	lt red
△	721	◣		324	orange
+	727			293	yellow
-	754	▢		1012	flesh
●	797			132	dk blue
✳	798			131	blue
▲	909	◣		923	dk green
◇	913			204	green
☆	3716			25	pink

PATTERNS (continued)

RELISH CONTAINER
(Page 21)

JAR LID

FLOWERPOT

SEASHELL WREATH
ORNAMENT
(Page 24)

MOOSE
WRAPPING PAPER
AND TAG
(Page 35)

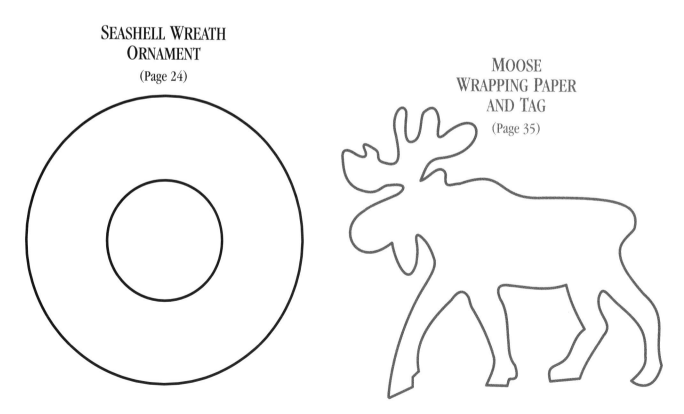

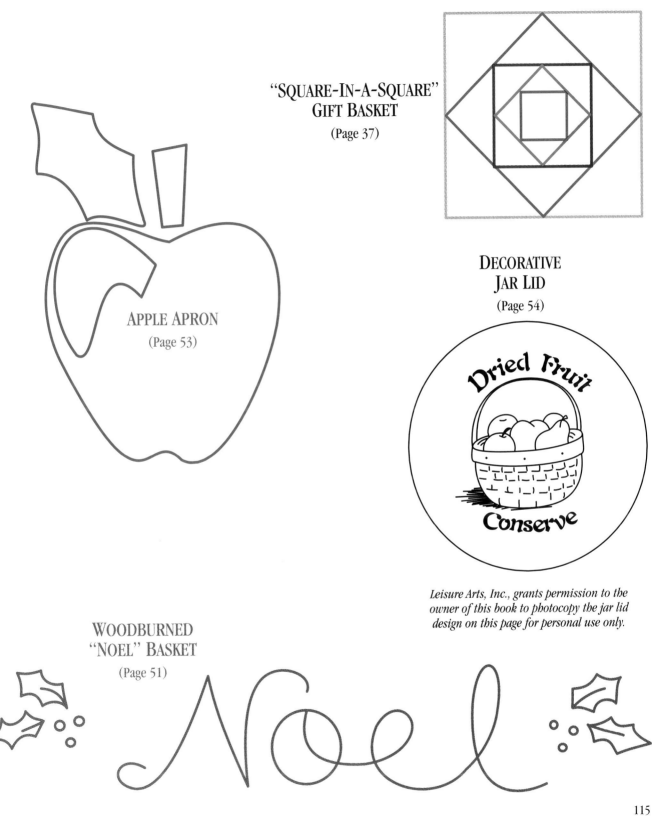

"SQUARE-IN-A-SQUARE" GIFT BASKET

(Page 37)

APPLE APRON

(Page 53)

DECORATIVE JAR LID

(Page 54)

Dried Fruit Conserve

Leisure Arts, Inc., grants permission to the owner of this book to photocopy the jar lid design on this page for personal use only.

WOODBURNED "NOEL" BASKET

(Page 51)

Noel

PATTERNS (continued)

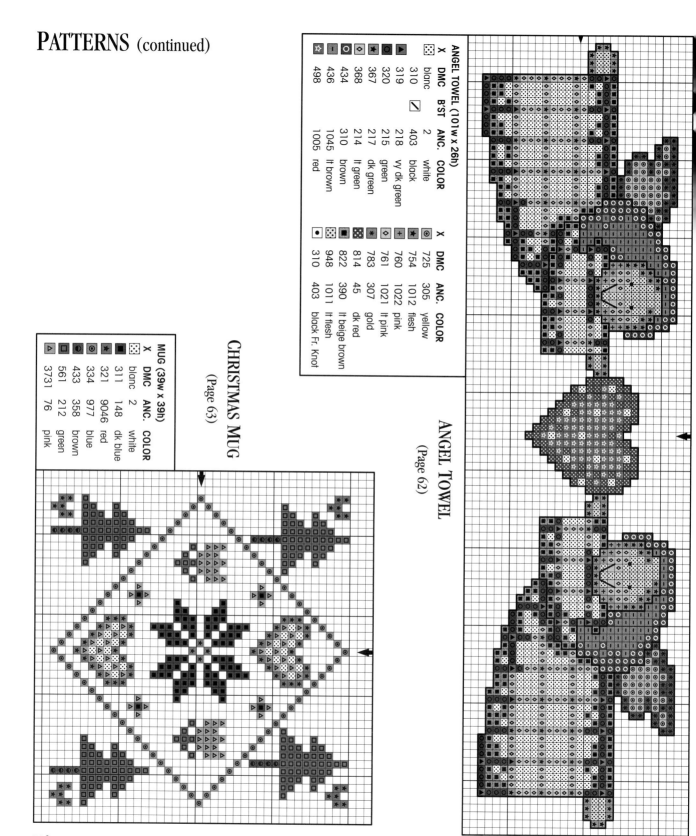

ANGEL TOWEL (101w x 26h)

X	DMC	B'ST	ANC.	COLOR
☆	blanc		2	white
I	310	◿	403	black
●	319		218	vy dk green
◇	320		215	green
★	367		217	dk green
◎	368		214	lt green
▶	434		310	brown
	436		1045	lt brown
	498		1005	red

X	DMC	ANC.	COLOR
●	725	305	yellow
▨	754	1012	flesh
■	760	1022	pink
▦	761	1021	lt pink
✳	783	307	gold
◇	814	45	dk red
+	822	390	lt beige brown
★	948	1011	lt flesh
◉	310	403	black Fr. Knot

ANGEL TOWEL
(Page 62)

CHRISTMAS MUG
(Page 63)

MUG (39w x 39h)

X	DMC	ANC.	COLOR
▷	blanc	2	white
□	311	148	dk blue
◐	321	9046	red
◉	334	977	blue
★	433	358	brown
■	561	212	green
▨	3731	76	pink

116

REINDEER
ORNAMENT

(Page 71)

STENCIL CUTTING KEY
Stencil #1
Stencil #2

COLOR KEY
Stencil #1 — tan with gold shading
Stencil #2 — green

COUNTRY
GIFT SACKS

(Page 59)

PATTERNS (continued)

SPOON-TOPPED GIFT SACKS
(Page 76)

"FELIZ NAVIDAD" DISH
(Page 81)

☆ Feliz Navidad ◎

FESTIVE BAG
(Page 82)

SUNFLOWER SNOWMAN BAG
(Page 85)

HEARTWARMING TAG
(Page 87)

warm hearts
warm wishes

GINGERBREAD BOY PINS
(Page 94)

HEART APPLIQUÉ BAG
(Page 95)

SNOWMAN TAG
(Page 99)

PATTERNS (continued)

GINGERBREAD MAN
TAG
(Page 104)

CHRISTMAS TOTES
(Page 105)

COOKIE BASKET
(Page 111)

Recipe for
snowman
cookies

snowman
cookie
kit

button
up.!

eyes
for
you!

to:
from:

warm
clothes!

cold
nose.!

GENERAL INSTRUCTIONS

TRACING PATTERNS

Place tracing paper over pattern and trace pattern; cut out. For a more durable pattern, use a permanent pen to trace pattern onto acetate; cut out.

ABOUT THE PAPER WE USED

For many of the projects in this book, we used white and colored paper. There are a variety of papers available at copy centers or craft stores for these projects. When selecting paper, choose one that is suitable in weight for the project. We used copier paper, card and cover stock, construction paper, poster board, and bristol board.

GLUES

Use the following guidelines to decide which glue or glues to use for your project. Carefully follow manufacturer's instructions when using any kind of glue.

WHITE CRAFT GLUE: Recommended for paper. Dry flat.

TACKY CRAFT GLUE: Recommended for paper, fabric, florals, or wood. Dry flat or secure items with clothespins or straight pins until glue is dry.

CRAFT GLUE STICK: Recommended for paper or for gluing small, lightweight items to paper or another surface. Dry flat.

FABRIC GLUE: Recommended for fabric or paper. Dry flat or secure items with clothespins or straight pins until glue is dry.

DECOUPAGE GLUE: Recommended for decoupaging fabric or paper to a surface such as wood or glass. Use purchased decoupage glue or mix 1 part craft glue with 1 part water.

HOT OR LOW-TEMPERATURE GLUE GUN: Recommended for florals, paper, fabric, or wood. Hold in place until set. A low-temperature glue gun is safer than a hot glue gun, but the bond made with the glue is not as strong.

RUBBER CEMENT: Recommended for paper and cardboard. May discolor photos; may discolor paper with age. Dry flat (dries very quickly).

SPRAY ADHESIVE: Recommended for paper or fabric. Can be repositionable or permanent. Dry flat.

MAKING APPLIQUÉS

1. (*Note*: When tracing patterns for more than 1 appliqué, leave at least 1" between shapes on web. To make a reverse appliqué, trace pattern onto tracing paper, turn traced pattern over, and follow all steps using traced pattern.) Trace appliqué pattern onto paper side of web. Cutting about $1/2$" outside drawn lines, cut out web shape.
2. Fuse web shape to wrong side of fabric. Cut out shape along drawn lines.

SPONGE PAINTING

Place project on a newspaper-covered work surface. Practice sponge painting technique on scrap paper until desired look is achieved. Use an assembly-line approach when making several sponge-painted projects. Paint all projects with first color before changing to second color. Use a clean sponge for each additional color.

ALLOVER SPONGE PAINTING: Dip sponge piece into paint; remove excess paint on a paper towel. Use a light stamping motion to paint project; allow to dry.

PAINTING WITH SPONGE SHAPES: Dip sponge shape into paint; remove excess paint on a paper towel. Lightly press sponge shape onto project. Carefully lift sponge. Reapplying paint as necessary, repeat. For a reverse design, turn sponge shape over.

STENCILING

1. (*Note:* These instructions are written for multicolor stencils. For single-color stencils, make 1 stencil for entire design.) For first stencil, cut a piece of acetate 1" larger than entire pattern. Center acetate over pattern and use pen to trace outlines of all areas of first color in stencil cutting key. For placement guidelines, outline remaining colored areas using dashed lines. Using a new piece of acetate for each additional color in stencil cutting key, repeat for remaining stencils.
2. Place each acetate piece on cutting mat and use craft knife to cut out stencil along solid lines, making sure edges are smooth.
3. Hold or tape stencil in place. Use a clean, dry stencil brush or sponge piece. Dip brush or sponge in paint; remove excess paint on a paper towel. Brush or sponge should be almost dry to produce good results. Beginning at edge of cutout area, apply paint in a stamping motion over stencil. If desired, highlight or shade design by stamping a lighter or darker shade of paint in cutout area. Repeat until all areas of first stencil have been painted. Carefully remove stencil and allow paint to dry.
4. Using stencils in order indicated in color key and matching guidelines on stencils to previously stenciled areas, repeat Step 3 for remaining stencils.

Continued on page 122

GENERAL INSTRUCTIONS (continued)

CROSS STITCH

COUNTED CROSS STITCH(X)

Work 1 Cross Stitch to correspond to each colored square in chart. For horizontal rows, work stitches in 2 journeys (Fig. 1). For vertical rows, complete each stitch as shown in Fig. 2. When working over 2 fabric threads, work Cross Stitch as shown in Fig. 3. When chart shows a Backstitch crossing a colored square (Fig. 4), a Cross Stitch (Fig. 1, 2, or 3) should be worked first, then Backstitch (Fig. 6) should be worked on top of Cross Stitch.

Fig. 1

Fig. 2

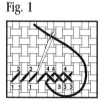

Fig. 3

Fig. 4

QUARTER STITCH(¼X)

Quarter Stitches are denoted by triangular shapes of color in chart and color key. Come up at 1 (Fig. 5), then split fabric thread to go down at 2.

Fig. 5

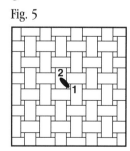

BACKSTITCH(B'ST)

For outline detail, Backstitch (shown in chart and color key by black or colored straight lines) should be worked after design has been completed (Fig. 6).

Fig. 6

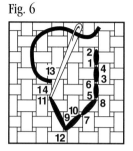

FRENCH KNOT

Bring needle up at 1. Wrap floss once around needle and take needle down at 2, holding end of floss with non-stitching fingers (Fig. 7). Tighten knot, then pull needle through fabric, holding floss until it must be released. For a larger knot, use more strands; wrap only once.

Fig. 7

CROCHET

SINGLE CROCHET

Insert hook in stitch or space indicated, YO and pull up a loop, YO and draw through both loops on hook (Fig. 1).

Fig. 1

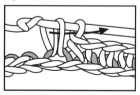

DOUBLE CROCHET

YO, insert hook in stitch or space indicated, YO and pull up a loop, YO and draw through 2 loops on hook (Fig. 2). YO and draw through remaining 2 loops on hook (Fig. 3).

Fig. 2

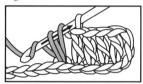

Fig. 3

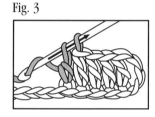

JAR LID FINISHING

1. For jar lid insert, use flat part of a jar lid (same size as jar lid used in storing food) as a pattern and cut 1 circle each from cardboard, batting, and fabric. Use craft glue to glue batting circle to cardboard circle. Center fabric circle right side up on batting; glue edges of fabric circle to batting.

2. (*Caution:* If jar has been sealed in canning, be careful not to break seal of lid while following Step 2. If seal of lid is broken, jar must be refrigerated.) Just before presenting gift, remove band from filled jar; place jar lid insert in band and replace band over lid.

MAKING A MULTI-LOOP BOW

1. For first streamer, measure desired length of streamer from 1 end of ribbon and gather ribbon between fingers (Fig. 1). For first loop, keep right side facing out and fold ribbon over to form desired size loop (Fig. 2). Repeat to form another loop same size as first loop (Fig. 3). Repeat to form desired number of loops. For remaining streamer, trim ribbon to desired length.

Fig. 1   Fig. 2   Fig. 3

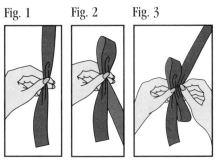

2. To secure bow, hold gathered loops tightly. Wrap a length of wire around center. Hold wire ends behind bow, gathering loops forward; twist bow to tighten wire. Arrange loops as desired.
3. For bow center, wrap a 6" length of ribbon around center of bow, covering wire and overlapping ends at back; trim excess. Glue to secure.
4. Trim ribbon ends as desired.

MAKING A TAG

Photocopy one of the tag designs on this page, color and personalize it, then cut it out and attach it to your gift. For extra color, glue the tag to a piece of colored paper before attaching it to your gift.

MAKING A FABRIC-BACKED TAG

Fuse web to back of paper and fabric for tag. Cut paper desired size. Fuse fabric to poster board. Fuse paper piece to fabric-covered poster board. Trim fabric-covered poster board to desired size.

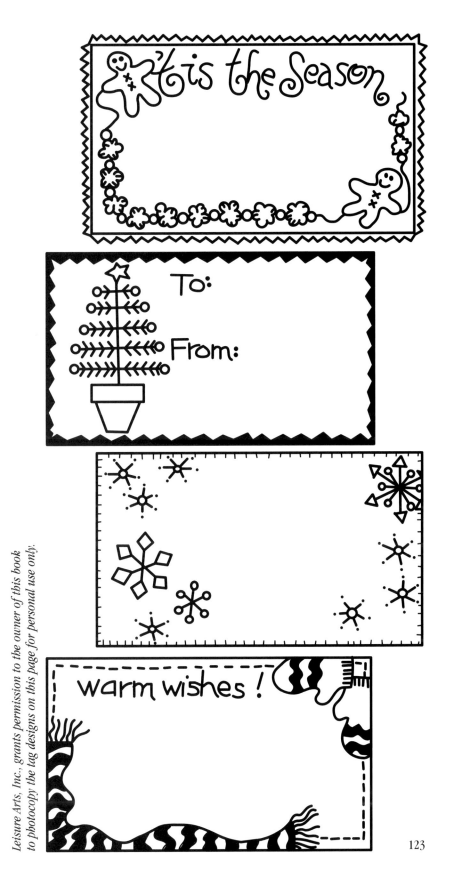

KITCHEN TIPS

MEASURING INGREDIENTS

Liquid measuring cups have a rim above the measuring line to keep liquid ingredients from spilling. Nested measuring cups are used to measure dry ingredients, butter, shortening, and peanut butter. Measuring spoons are used for measuring both dry and liquid ingredients.

To measure flour or granulated sugar: Spoon ingredient into nested measuring cup and level off with a knife. Do not pack down with spoon.

To measure confectioners sugar: Sift sugar, spoon lightly into nested measuring cup, and level off with a knife.

To measure brown sugar: Pack sugar into nested measuring cup and level off with a knife. Sugar should hold its shape when removed from cup.

To measure dry ingredients equaling less than $1/4$ cup: Dip measuring spoon into ingredient and level off with a knife.

To measure butter, shortening, or peanut butter: Pack ingredient firmly into nested measuring cup and level off with a knife.

To measure liquids: Use a liquid measuring cup placed on a flat surface. Pour ingredient into cup and check measuring line at eye level.

To measure honey or syrup: For a more accurate measurement, lightly spray measuring cup or spoon with cooking spray before measuring so the liquid will release easily from cup or spoon.

TESTS FOR CANDY MAKING

To determine the correct temperature of cooked candy, use a candy thermometer and the cold water test. Before each use, check the accuracy of your candy thermometer by attaching it to the side of a small saucepan of water, making sure thermometer does not touch bottom of pan. Bring water to a boil. Thermometer should register 212 degrees in boiling water. If it does not, adjust the temperature range for each candy consistency accordingly.

When using a candy thermometer, insert thermometer into candy mixture, making sure thermometer does not touch bottom of pan. Read temperature at eye level. Cook candy to desired temperature range. Working quickly, drop about $1/2$ teaspoon of candy mixture into a cup of ice water. Use a fresh cup of water for each test. Use the following descriptions to determine if candy has reached the correct consistency:

Soft Ball Stage (234 to 240 degrees): Candy can be rolled into a soft ball in ice water but will flatten when held in your hand.

Firm Ball Stage (242 to 248 degrees): Candy can be rolled into a firm ball in ice water but will flatten if pressed when removed from the water.

Hard Ball Stage (250 to 268 degrees): Candy can be rolled into a hard ball in ice water and will remain hard when removed from the water.

Soft Crack Stage (270 to 290 degrees): Candy will form hard threads in ice water but will soften when removed from the water.

Hard Crack Stage (300 to 310 degrees): Candy will form brittle threads in ice water and will remain brittle when removed from the water.

TOASTING NUTS

To toast nuts, spread nuts on an ungreased baking sheet. Stirring occasionally, bake in a 350-degree oven 5 to 8 minutes or until nuts are slightly darker in color.

PREPARING CITRUS FRUIT ZEST

To remove the zest (colored outer portion of peel) from citrus fruits, use a fine grater or fruit zester, being careful not to grate white portion of peel, which is bitter.

MELTING CHOCOLATE

To melt chocolate, place chopped or shaved chocolate in top of a double boiler over hot, not boiling, water. Stir occasionally until chocolate melts. Remove from heat and use as desired. If necessary, chocolate may be returned to heat to remelt.

SHREDDING CHEESE

To shred cheese easily, place wrapped cheese in freezer 10 to 20 minutes before shredding.

SOFTENING BUTTER OR MARGARINE

To soften 1 stick of butter, remove wrapper and place butter on a microwave-safe plate. Microwave on medium-low power (30%) 20 to 30 seconds.

SOFTENING CREAM CHEESE

To soften cream cheese, remove wrapper and place cream cheese on a microwave-safe plate. Microwave on medium power (50%) 1 to $1 1/2$ minutes for an 8-ounce package or 30 to 45 seconds for a 3-ounce package.

WHIPPING CREAM

For greatest volume, chill a glass bowl, beaters, and cream before whipping. In warm weather, place chilled bowl over ice while whipping cream.

TOASTING COCONUT

To toast coconut, spread a thin layer of coconut on an ungreased baking sheet.

Stirring occasionally, bake 5 to 7 minutes in a 350-degree oven or until coconut is lightly browned.

MAKING SUPERFINE SUGAR

Superfine sugar is preferred in some recipes because it dissolves quickly and gives a better texture. Process granulated sugar in a food processor until it becomes a fine powder. Use the same amount as granulated sugar.

MELTING CANDY COATING

To melt candy coating, place in top of a double boiler over hot, not boiling, water or in a heavy saucepan over low heat. Stir occasionally with a dry spoon until coating melts. Remove from heat and use for dipping as desired. To flavor candy coating, add a small amount of flavored oil. To thin coating, add a small amount of vegetable oil, but no water. If necessary, coating may be returned to heat to remelt.

EQUIVALENT MEASUREMENTS

1 tablespoon	=	3 teaspoons
$1/8$ cup (1 fluid ounce)	=	2 tablespoons
$1/4$ cup (2 fluid ounces)	=	4 tablespoons
$1/3$ cup	=	$5 1/3$ tablespoons
$1/2$ cup (4 fluid ounces)	=	8 tablespoons
$3/4$ cup (6 fluid ounces)	=	12 tablespoons
1 cup (8 fluid ounces)	=	16 tablespoons or $1/2$ pint
2 cups (16 fluid ounces)	=	1 pint
1 quart (32 fluid ounces)	=	2 pints
$1/2$ gallon (64 fluid ounces)	=	2 quarts
1 gallon (128 fluid ounces)	=	4 quarts

HELPFUL FOOD EQUIVALENTS

$1/2$ cup butter	=	1 stick butter
1 square baking chocolate	=	1 ounce chocolate
1 cup chocolate chips	=	6 ounces chocolate chips
$2 1/4$ cups packed brown sugar	=	1 pound brown sugar
$3 1/2$ cups unsifted confectioners sugar	=	1 pound confectioners sugar
2 cups granulated sugar	=	1 pound granulated sugar
4 cups all-purpose flour	=	1 pound all-purpose flour
1 cup shredded cheese	=	4 ounces cheese
3 cups sliced carrots	=	1 pound carrots
$1/2$ cup chopped celery	=	1 rib celery
$1/2$ cup chopped onion	=	1 medium onion
1 cup chopped green pepper	=	1 large green pepper

RECIPE INDEX

CREDITS

To Magna IV Color Imaging of Little Rock, Arkansas, we say *thank you* for the superb color reproduction and excellent pre-press preparation.

We want to especially thank photographers Larry Pennington, Mark Mathews, Ken West, and Karen Shirey of Peerless Photography, Little Rock, Arkansas, and Jerry R. Davis of Jerry Davis Photography, Little Rock, Arkansas, for their time, patience, and excellent work.

To the talented people who helped in the creation of the following recipe and projects in this book, we extend a special word of thanks:

- *Elf Ornament*, page 20: Terrie Lee Steinmeyer
- *Angel Towel*, page 62: Jane Chandler
- *Christmas Mug*, page 63: Polly Carbonari
- *Heavenly Bars*, page 73: Sherry Sanders
- *Crocheted Pot Holder*, page 87: Joan Beebe

Our sincere appreciation also goes to Elaine Garrett, who assisted in making and testing some of the projects in this book.